To

July 5.th 1956.

ACTION IN CRICKET

GODFREY EVANS' RECORDS

Has played in more Tests than any other wicket-keeper (66 to date).

Has obtained more Test victims than any other 'keeper (147).

Is the only stumper to dismiss 100 victims and score 1,500 runs in Test cricket.

Has played in more Tests than any other Kent cricketer.

His 115 catches in Test cricket surpasses the previous record of 89 held by Walter Hammond.

Holds the world's record for not conceding a bye while 1,054 runs were scored (Australia, 1946).

Claims more victims than any other contemporary County 'keeper.

In 1947 obtained 93 victims and scored 1,100 runs (his nearest approach to the wicket-keeper's " double ").

Has two Test centuries (104 *v.* India, and 104 *v.* West Indies).

The only living English wicket-keeper to score the winning hit in a Test series in Australia (1955).

Holds the record for the longest Test innings without scoring (95 minutes *v.* Australia, at Adelaide, 1947).

Jointly holds the fastest score before lunch in a Test match with Charlie Barnett (98 *v.* India, at Lord's, 1952).

ACTION IN CRICKET

GODFREY EVANS

With a Foreword by
PETER MAY

LONDON
HODDER AND STOUGHTON

FIRST PRINTED 1956

Made and Printed in Great Britain for Hodder and
Stoughton Limited, London, by Butler and Tanner
Limited, Frome and London

Foreword

IT IS A GREAT PLEASURE TO WRITE A FOREWORD TO THIS book, for there can be no doubt that its author is one of the greatest wicket-keepers of any era.

To me, and to any side, it is always a wonderful tonic to have Godfrey Evans on the field with one. You will read of his skill behind the stumps, and his uncanny anticipation of the most unsuspecting leg glance, but I think it is his enthusiasm and boundless energy that impress me most. At the end of the hottest day in Australia or the West Indies he would keep us on our toes by his inspiring example, and I shall never forget the look he gave me when I threw an impossible return past him to the boundary. I can assure you that the next one was right on the mark !

During the last tour of Australia, when we retained the Ashes, Godfrey produced his own slogan in the dressing-room when things seemed to be at their worst for us : " Don't worry," he would say, " we shall be there at the finish." He certainly fulfilled this at Adelaide by applying the *coup de grâce* himself with one of his own special strokes that settled the rubber.

Energy and purposeful action symbolise his batting— the Indians will always remember him at Lord's !—and there are few batsmen quicker than he between the wickets. But if you imagine that this amazing vitality of his ends on the cricket field, you should see him perform his own type of " German Band " at a party.

I know that you will enjoy this book, for Godfrey Evans is a likeable and inspiring personality. May he continue to display his magic behind the stumps for many years to come.

PETER MAY

5

THE HODDER & STOUGHTON CRICKET BOOKS

Godfrey Evans
BEHIND THE STUMPS

Alec Bedser
BOWLING

Don Bradman
FAREWELL TO CRICKET
HOW TO PLAY CRICKET

Jack Cheetham
CAUGHT BY THE SPRINGBOKS
I DECLARE

Dudley Nourse
CRICKET IN THE BLOOD

E. W. Swanton
ELUSIVE VICTORY
CRICKET AND THE CLOCK

Roy Webber
THE AUSTRALIANS IN ENGLAND
WHO'S WHO IN WORLD CRICKET

Ian Peebles
THE ASHES 1954–1955

Contents

Key to illustration acknowledgements :

(1) Allan Studios, Victoria, Australia
(2) Howard R. Boase, Glandore, S. Australia
(3) Central Press Photos Ltd., London
(4) Pierre Chong, Kingston, Jamaica
(5) *Daily News*, Australia
(6) *Kentish Gazette* Photographic Service
(7) *Kent Messenger*
(8) Photo-Reportage Ltd., London
(9) The Sport & General Press Agency Ltd., London
(10) W.A. Newspapers Ltd., Perth, W. Australia

8

List of Illustrations

CHAPTER I

Let's Look Back—and Forward

IN THE EARLY PART OF MY CAREER, ENGLAND'S FORTUNES in the field of international cricket were at a low ebb, due to six years of hostilities in World War II. This robbed the game of stars who no doubt would have kept England in the forefront of the cricketing world, and also severely handicapped the development of the younger men.

The immediate post-war years were difficult in the extreme, and England relied mainly on three or four of the leading stars of pre-war days. Upon the shoulders of these men fell the full responsibility of acting as the foundation on which was built the side that was to rise within a few short years to a position at the head of the cricketing world.

In my previous book, *Behind the Stumps*, I wrote of my earlier experiences and of how I attained one of my ambitions—to play for England on Test fields, for I was one of those younger players privileged to help in the foundation and build-up of the side that holds such high ranking today.

Much has happened in the world of cricket since that time, and I now want to give you my views and opinions on why England's fortunes have blossomed into such a healthy condition following that rather bleak and disappointing period.

During this same period of England's ascendancy, however, Australia's cricket supremacy was on the decline, due in no small measure to the retirement of the illustrious Sir Donald Bradman and many of the outstanding personalities in that wonderful cricketing machine that was almost unbeatable in the immediate post-war years.

How does one account for this change of fortune in so

short a time ?   Is it the interest created in cricket in the Counties that has helped to develop such a high standard in the younger generation ?   Or is the mere fact that because of lack of playing facilities, young England had no opportunity to develop until the six lean years of wartime had passed ?   Do I think it is the entry into the Test lime-light of two great fast bowlers ?   Or is it that we have now discovered two young batsmen in world class, to-gether with the continued brilliance of the already estab-lished stars, that has made our victories possible ?   Or, maybe, it is the healthy atmosphere of competition for places that is at the present time so apparent in England's happy position ?

The selectors now have a choice of players for almost all departments in the Test side, and maybe this position has come about by the fact that modern young players have so much more opportunity of getting the required practice and experience than was the case in the imme-diate period following the resumption of cricket after the war.

Competition for places—yes.   For instance, we have fast bowlers in Frank Tyson, Brian Statham, Alec Bedser, Peter Loader and Freddie Trueman ; for off-spin there are Bob Appleyard and Jim Laker ; for left arm there are Tony Lock and Johnny Wardle—and so I could go on. Never was competition for places so keen as it is today, and if this healthy state can continue, then English cricket will have no worries regarding the future, and our side will put up performances of which the country will be justly proud, and which the crowds will flock to see.

So far as the Australians are concerned, the reason for their surprising decline appears to be the lack of specialists in one department or the other.   During our recent series they had no less than six all-rounders forming the nucleus of their side.   This must mean a weakness in the make-up of any team, and although all-rounders in a side are a decided advantage, too many can spoil the balance of the team.

I mean by this that whereas in the past an all-rounder

like Keith Miller would come in to bat with the score at 350 for 5, today he has to face the bowling when the score is more likely to be about 20 for 2, a totally different proposition.

Another reason for Australia's decline I feel, is the revision of the new-ball rule. During the Bradman regime, a new ball could be taken after only 55 overs had been bowled. But a change to the 200 runs rule meant that the spinners came into their own, and it is in this field that, at the moment, Australia are struggling. Their major thrust in attack comes from the pace bowling of Lindwall and Miller, which has afforded little opportunity for the development of their spin bowlers. It is in this department of the game that England are now so much better equipped than the Australians.

Then again, Lindwall and Miller, although still great bowlers, cannot possibly be expected to produce such fire as they did in those illustrious years of Australian supremacy. On the other hand, we in England have found several really fine fast bowlers when a few years ago there appeared to be no prospect of finding even one. In those days our attack relied so much on the great-hearted Alec Bedser.

Just a personal note.

When I was in my 20's, I found my love of cricket so great that I could play every day and all day throughout the year if needs be. Since I have passed into the 30's, however, I find the strain much greater, and I am sure this does affect one's cricket at certain times during a season. The strain of international cricket in particular, is more severe than in the past, because we not only have the paying spectators and members in their thousands, but literally millions more watch in their homes through the medium of TV.

This aspect is made very apparent by the experience of our first and great professional captain Len Hutton, to whom the strain must have been tremendous, and undoubtedly has had much to do with his present ill-health. The same is true of Denis Compton, who in his youth played international football as well as cricket, and the strain of almost constant top-grade cricket during the post-war years has caused the knee trouble that has brought him so much pain.

Fortunately, the older you grow, the more experienced you become, and I find more and more how invaluable this experience is when the strain is on. It is this same experience in my own particular sphere behind the stumps that enables me to express freely and frankly my viewpoints of all the many and varied phases of cricket and cricketers as I have seen them during the last few years. I hope that the reading of some of these experiences and opinions in the ensuing pages of this book will bring entertainment and enjoyment to cricket lovers all over the world.

CHAPTER II

1950–51—Memories of Freddie Brown's Tour

W HEN I ADOPTED CRICKET AS MY PROFESSION, AND
gained my place as wicket-keeper in the Kent
County XI, after serving my " apprenticeship " with the
Colts and Minor Counties sides, I had two great ambitions. One was to play for England in a Test match,
the other to go to Australia. One man more than any
other inspired me, and that was Leslie Ames, England's
former Kent stumper, who was my boyhood idol. It was
Les who was among the first to congratulate me in 1946
when I was chosen to make my Test debut, against India,
and again when, on that unforgettable day in July 1946,
I heard of my selection as a member of the first post-war
team to tour Australia.

Little did I dream, or dare hope, that I should make
two further trips " Down Under ", and, eventually, be a
member of the team that would return with the Ashes.
But that memorable experience cannot be related yet.
First there was the 1950–51 tour, and although, as in
1946–47, we were unsuccessful in our quest for the Ashes,
that Test series provided me with yet another memorable
chapter in my cricket life.

It was certainly a happy tour under Freddie Brown,
who could not have done more to develop the right team
spirit and comradeship in the party from the moment we
met in London on the night before we sailed. I well
remember that first get-together at the Great Western
Hotel, Paddington, when Freddie spoke to us in that
charming way that was to make him so popular as captain.

" I shall be satisfied if we can win even a couple of
Tests," he said, " although there is no reason why we
should not bring back the Ashes."

There was an air of confidence about him that set the

whole tone of the tour, and the players were quick to respond, for we, like our captain, rather resented the almost contemptuous attitude of certain sections of the Press. The majority opinion was that we hadn't the ghost of a chance of winning even one Test. One scribe even went so far as to say that as we had no possible chance of winning, it seemed hopeless to send a team to Australia at all.

What a defeatist attitude. It certainly annoyed us, and we were whole-heartedly behind Freddie in accepting the challenge.

A great deal has happened since that day in 1950, so let me recall for you the players who were my colleagues on that tour :

Len Hutton, Denis Compton, Reg Simpson, Trevor Bailey, John Dewes, Gilbert Parkhouse, Brian Close, David Sheppard, Alec Bedser, Arthur McIntyre, Doug Wright, Bob Berry, Eric Hollies, John Warr, Freddie Brown and myself. Cyril Washbrook was among the original selections, but he did not accompany us on the voyage, flying out to join us later. Then, of course, Brian Statham and Roy Tattersall were sent for during the tour.

Some of those selected were not the men you and I might have chosen, but then no team has ever received universal approval. However, although our personal opinions may have differed, the selectors undoubtedly did their best to produce a side which they considered good enough to hold its own. We know now that it was not strong enough to recapture the Ashes, but I am sure that if the luck had gone our way, we might at least have drawn the series.

I was highly honoured when Freddie Brown, as captain, and Brigadier Green, as manager, invited me to join the Selection Committee for the tour, along with vice-captain Denis Compton, Len Hutton and Cyril Washbrook.

We were soon a happy party, and on the boat we formed the usual M.C.C. club. As on the previous tour, we had some wonderful times at our weekly " get-together " on Saturday evenings. These Saturday club-nights are a familiar feature of all M.C.C. touring sides. The boys have to get together every Saturday night for about half an hour in order to drink two toasts—1. To those at home ; and 2. To sweethearts and wives.

Another of the club rules is that every member must drink left-handed on Saturdays. Anyone found breaking the rules is fined 6d. Fines are also imposed for swearing, and anyone not wearing his M.C.C. tie on Monday mornings—that costs you half a crown ! All fines go into a pool which helps to pay for the Saturday evening club meetings.

I am all in favour of this club, for it helps to promote the happy family spirit. Then again, the Saturday evening meetings help us to forget the cricket—and our bad performances, if there are any, of course. At our meetings, too, any little differences of opinion that may crop up can be thrashed out in a happy atmosphere.

On the voyage out, we stopped at Colombo for a one-day match. I was nursing a damaged finger and could not play, so Arthur McIntyre kept wicket. He also hit a magnificent 100 in that match, and as I sat watching, I really thought that Arthur would be a success on the Australian wickets.

We thoroughly enjoyed our short stay in Colombo. The weather was absolutely perfect, and as usual the Colombo crowd showed their appreciation of the cricket in no uncertain manner. At the end of the match some students got so excited about the game that they set light to the pavilion, so the tour nearly ended in Colombo—well, that's not quite true, but very nearly !

We arrived in Australia at last—at Perth, as usual—and this must have been a great thrill for those members of the team who were making their first trip " Down Under ". It was a thrill to me, too—and, incidentally, it gave me a good laugh.

When an M.C.C. team arrive in Australia, the welcome is something to be remembered for all time. Among the great crowds thronging the quayside are those who have

2

been deputed to pick up individual players and conduct them to the team's hotel. It is a personal touch that is much appreciated. On this occasion, the bronzed Australian who was to be my guide and " chauffeur " stepped forward to greet me, and I recognised him at once. He was the same man who had picked me up on my previous visit in 1946, although he did not seem to remember it.

He greeted me in exactly the same way as before, and then asked me : " Would you like to see the wild flowers in King's Park ? " Yes, it was an exact repetition of his greeting on my previous visit.

I knew it was a beautiful drive, so, of course, I agreed. And then, as we drove through King's Park, my guide said :

" I am very sorry the wild flowers aren't out so much as they might be, but the season for wild flowers is a little late this year."

I could almost have repeated the words myself, for he had made exactly the same apology in 1946. It struck me as a little humorous at the time, although, of course, I do not want to appear ungracious. He was doing his best, and doing it right well, too. No English cricketer can ever complain about the hospitality of the Australians. The people out there cannot do enough for us when we are in their wonderful country.

Our lads quickly got down to work, and were soon showing great form with the bat. Arthur McIntyre had to look after the wicket-keeping, because of my damaged finger, which kept me out of action for quite a time. However, it was mending and I managed to keep in practice.

Our first success against a State side came when we played South Australia, in Adelaide. Phil Ridings, the South Australian captain, declared, leaving M.C.C. to score 185 in just over 100 minutes, which was quite within the powers of any touring side.

Freddie Brown gave the order to " go for 'em ", and we won that match with nearly 20 minutes to spare, after

Reg Simpson and Cyril Washbrook had put on over 130 for the second wicket. I recall the match very well because the skipper and I were together at the end, but when we still wanted 20 runs to win, Freddie strolled up to me and said : " Now look, we have got twenty minutes in which to get the runs, old boy, so we will get them in singles." However, this was not necessary. As luck would have it, the bowling just suited me and I hit five fours off the next six balls. The last of these fours took us to victory.

That is not quite all the story. Just before that over started, Phil Ridings said to Freddie : " Don't worry, Freddie, I'll give you a chance to get those runs. I'm going on myself next over ! " Well, the joke was on him, because he never got a chance.

During our early games against South Australia, Victoria and New South Wales the side was showing obvious signs of blending into a real team, although, of course, we had reached no decision concerning the selection of the side for the first Test. But after two more drawn games, against Victoria and N.S.W., we went up-country for two-day matches in Newcastle and Lismore. Both games were drawn and these results brought some rather severe criticism from the Press.

I played against the N.S.W. country team at Newcastle, and I can assure you we had rather a struggle against a side with a great fighting spirit. One day was rained off and, therefore, we virtually had to finish it in one day. We lost on the first innings and the critics began to write us off as a poor side. Freddie Brown particularly came in for a lot of criticism for leaving Len Hutton, Cyril Washbrook and Denis Compton back in Sydney in order to give experience to the younger players, Sheppard, Parkhouse, Dewes and Warr and one or two others.

Naturally, the country sides and their followers were disappointed at not seeing Len Hutton, Denis Compton and Cyril Washbrook, but on a long and arduous tour the captain must study the side as a whole. After all, the younger players in the party were out there for experience, and I think Freddie was quite right in giving the "juniors" a chance to play. It is physically impossible for any man to play in every match of any tour. In any case, it is only fair for the outstanding players—those on whom rests the main burden in the Tests—to be rested whenever possible.

Our next game, against Queensland, was yet another draw, mainly owing to a whole day being wasted because of rain—and that took us to the first Test !

The selectors went into a huddle to decide on the team ; no easy matter, I can assure you. At last we announced our choice, and the selection of Arthur McIntyre, my recognised deputy, as a batsman, seemed to come as a great surprise. I could never understand why. As a selection committee, we had no hesitation in making our decision, for Arthur was batting very well at the time. We knew, too, that he made a real effort to get on with the game, as he does today in County cricket for Surrey. When Arthur McIntyre gets runs, he gets them very quickly. It is always a great asset to have a No. 7, 8 or 9 in the side who can attack the bowling, and as we were rather short of batsmen who could really attack, we felt justified in including him in the team for the first Test.

Unfortunately, Freddie lost the toss, and with Lindsay Hassett electing to take first knock on a wonderful batting wicket we felt our luck was out. But you may recall that we surprised everybody—apparently !—by bowling Australia out for 228. Alec Bedser bowled magnificently, getting 4 for 45, while Trevor Bailey backed him up wonderfully.

Jack Moroney opened for Australia with Arthur Morris, and he was out third ball of the match, caught by Len Hutton off Trevor Bailey. That put us right on top.

Neil Harvey was top scorer ; he batted beautifully for 74, but apart from Ray Lindwall, who gave one of his usual dashing displays and got a quick 40, no one else really got going. Our bowling was supported by some really inspired fielding. Our catching was all that it

should be and the ground fielding was grand. It was a
display that showed the Australians that we were not
the " easy meat " the Press had expected us to be.

Well, that was the first day, but then came rain, drench-
ing floods of storm rain, such as only Brisbane can produce. We had rain at Brisbane in 1946, and now here it
was again in 1950.

There was no possible chance of any play on the Saturday : in fact there was no resumption until just before
lunch on the Monday, and by that time, the Brisbane
wicket was a real " sticky dog ". I remember Freddie
sending in Reg Simpson and Cyril Washbrook, and it was
quickly obvious that the wicket was more than a bit lively
so I was sent in first wicket down in the hope that I could
snatch a few quick runs before the bowlers really took
command. However, I made only 16, and with the
score at 52 for 3, things began to happen. When we were
68 for 7, Freddie decided to declare. His idea, of course,
was to get Australia in on this horror of a wicket.

It was now our turn to enjoy the fun. Bailey and
Bedser were the only two bowlers used, and Australia
were 32 for 7 when *they* declared. But by now the wicket
was getting a little easier—or so we thought—and we felt
that 193 runs wanted for victory was not beyond us. But
hardly had the innings started, than we suffered a tremendous blow. Lindwall's first ball, a straight yorker to
Reg Simpson, hit the wicket, and that was that ! It was
bad luck for Reg, but it was a beautiful delivery, perfectly
timed as only Ray can do it, and it deserved to take a
wicket. That put us on our mettle a bit, and " play
safe " was the order. It was also decided to keep Len
Hutton and Denis Compton back in the hope that we
would not lose many wickets that night, so that Len and
Denis would be able to bat the following day when there
was every hope that the wicket would roll out well.

Matters did not quite work out, however, for in actual
fact we lost 6 wickets that night—Trevor Bailey hit a long
hop to Bill Johnston at square leg, Alec Bedser was
caught at deep mid-off and the last straw was when

Arthur McIntyre was run out trying for a fourth run two minutes before close of play. All were trying to play out time, but anxiety caused them to make mistakes.

That run-out was a brilliant piece of work by Bill Johnston. Incidentally, he was once a baseball thrower, and at one time I think held the junior record for throwing the cricket ball. Anyway, he threw the ball right from the boundary, a little wide of the stumps. Don Tallon raced across, caught it and from at least ten yards, threw down the wicket with Arthur McIntyre an inch out of his ground. It was bad luck for Arthur, but I was in with him at the time and when he called me, I had to back him up. No man should be run out at such a crucial stage of the game, but it is all too easy to be wise after the event.

Well, we were 6 wickets down for 40 and Len and I went in to continue the battle the following morning. The wicket played well, but then Bill Johnston came on, and he got me and then Denis caught off nearly successive balls at short leg by Sam Loxton. That was virtually the end, and we lost by 70 runs.

It might have been far worse, but for Len Hutton. Going in low down he finished with 62 not out. Master from the start of his fighting innings, he played beautifully, scoring freely with leg cuts and wonderful cover drives. He really was the Len Hutton we all know. Throughout the whole tour he showed us some of the most scintillating batting that had been seen in Australia from any cricketer —including the great Bradman himself. Len had everything—delightful shots through the covers, hooks, late cuts, and, when necessary, typical dour Yorkshire defence as well. If ever I admired Len, I did on the 1950–51 tour.

That first Test defeat at Brisbane was a severe disappointment for us all, but at least we felt we had shown that we were not lacking in fighting qualities and would not go down easily next time.

From Brisbane we went to Melbourne for the second Test, and Freddie lost the toss again. Australia elected to bat, and after we had taken our first look at the wicket which was very green, we were not sorry that we were fielding.

I have never seen Alec Bedser bowl with so much fire and move the ball about so much as he did on that first day of the second Test at Melbourne. On reflection I would say that this was one of Alec Bedser's best performances. He bowled 19 eight-ball overs and took 4 for 37, and it could easily have been 8, for in the humid atmosphere the ball was swinging in the air and moving about the pitch so devastatingly that he had even Neil Harvey in trouble. Actually, if I had not been keeping wicket absolutely at the top of my form, I could easily have given away about 40 byes, so much was the ball moving off the pitch. I was indeed lucky to get away with only 4 byes !

Thanks to Alec and Trevor Bailey we bowled Australia out for just 194 on the first day, and for the second time we had dismissed Hassett's men for under 250 runs after losing the toss. It gave us the encouragement we needed, and we thought : " If we can't get the runs this time, we will never be able to do it."

Next morning we started our innings, but our hopes were not entirely fulfilled, and wickets were soon falling. Luck was not exactly on our side, however, and I remember that Len Hutton was out to a bad decision. He took his bat away from a ball from Jack Iverson and let the ball hit the pad. It bounced up in the air and Don Tallon whipped round and caught it. But there was no excitement until someone half-heartedly appealed—and the umpire gave him out. It was a very great disappointment for Len and most disheartening for us in the pavilion to see him given out in that unsatisfactory way.

It seemed to have a bad effect on some of the other batsmen, although Freddie Brown did not let it affect him. He hit a magnificent 62, banging the ball all over the field. His merry knock gave us a fighting chance and, incidentally, I managed to hit 49, my highest Test score in Australia. We drew level with Australia's score and I tried to hit a four that would put us in front. Unfortunately, I was caught by Ian Johnson on the square leg boundary. Eventually, we did just get our noses in front, but not sufficiently to compensate for the advantage of bowling Australia out so cheaply on the first day. However, we still had a fighting chance.

In went Australia once more—and out they went again, this time for 181. Grand fielding and catching did much to make this possible, with Skipper Freddie Brown setting a most enthusiastic example. But then he fielded brilliantly throughout the whole tour. For a big chap, he was wonderfully agile.

At Melbourne the fielding of the whole side reached a very high standard indeed, and helped to give us a real chance of victory, for we needed to score only 178 to win. As you know, we failed by 28 runs.

I should be the last to make excuses, but if you remember, Denis Compton could not play because of a bad knee —that same knee that has caused him so much trouble during recent years. It was a great shame really, for if Denis had been in anything like his normal form, I am sure we should have got the runs and been home and dry. However, " ifs " do not win Test matches.

Not that there was any despondency in the English camp, for although we had lost the first two Tests, we knew we could have won either—or both—of those games, if only the luck had gone our way. I know we lost the first, at Brisbane, by 70 runs, but there was only 28 in it at Melbourne, hence our optimism as we approached the third Test at Sydney.

Here we won the toss, and things looked brighter than ever when we started off well, and the runs began to mount up. But then, when I was batting with Trevor Bailey, he played a Lindwall bouncer right behind the line of the ball. It hit his thumb and broke it. That was a sad blow, because he was our opening bowler, and with a broken thumb he could hardly hold the bat, even though he tried to struggle on for a time with the damaged member in plaster.

This was not the end of our misfortunes. Worse was to come.

When Doug Wright came in, I tried to pinch a short single to keep the bowling, but in trying to beat the ball as it whipped in from the field, Doug tore a muscle in his leg and was run out.

That was just about the crowning blow. With two established bowlers out of action, we were left with only Freddie Brown, John Warr and Alec Bedser. That did not allow for much variation against that great Australian run-getting machine, and, of course, we were soon right up against it.

The Australians scored at a pretty good rate the following day, and although our fielding was still very good, which kept the runs at a minimum, there was little we could do to restrain the batsmen. The three bowlers stuck to their disheartening task as well as they could, but it was too much for them.

After two whole days in the field—two rather exhausting days, we batted again. The wicket began to wear, and on the last day, Jack Iverson, with his freakish off-spin-come-googly-come-leg-spin bowling, on a turning wicket, took six of our wickets, and we lost by an innings. It was a great disappointment to us all, but the boys put up a gallant performance in the face of all our misfortunes. Yet with only three bowlers, it was almost inevitable that we should be on the losing end.

After those three Test defeats, Freddie Brown took a well-earned rest, and when we travelled across to Tasmania, Denis Compton took over the captaincy. He strode right back into cracking form with 142 at Launceston against the Australian XI, who were strengthened by the inclusion of Arthur Morris. This meant that Alec Bedser would get another chance of working his " hoodoo " on Arthur, and you can be sure that Alec was keen to get at his " rabbit ".

I remember an amusing incident that marked the friendly battle of wits between these two grand cricketers. As Denis Compton was setting the field for the start of the Australian innings, he said to Alec :

" Do you want me fine or wide at first slip, Alec ? "

" I'd better have you wide, skipper," said Alec.

The first ball he bowled to Arthur Morris was an absolute beauty. It swung away very late and Arthur, playing a half-forward shot, got a thin edge. The ball shot away past Denis' right hand for four runs.

Up went Alec's arms, saying : " You lucky old So-and-so, Arthur ! "

" You shouldn't bowl such tripe, Alec ! " Arthur laughed in reply.

As Denis Compton retrieved the ball, he said to Alec : " Now what do you want, Alec ? "

" You'd better go a bit finer," Alec suggested, so Denis took up his position a little closer to me.

Two balls later, Alec bowled another beauty. This time, Arthur lunged forward to cover the swing, and got a thick edge. The ball shot past Denis' outstretched LEFT hand for another four.

Alec was livid, and when Denis threw the ball back he said :

" Well, what do you want now, Alec ? "

" Get another blooming fielder ! Send twelfth man out—you're no good ! " was Alec's grumbling reply.

Naturally, this was all in good fun—and the man who enjoyed it most of all was Arthur Morris. But, as usual, it was Alec Bedser who had the last laugh. Yes, he got Arthur's wicket before he had added to his score !

The two matches in Tasmania are always most interesting. This delightful island resembles the English countryside more than any other place in Australia. Its greenery, its trees, and its charming people remind one so much of England, and it is always a treat to go there. The two matches also provide us with a little relaxation, for although they are regarded as first class, they are played in a very quiet and restful atmosphere, so different from the strain and tension of the Test matches.

Don't forget, 60,000 watch the cricket at Melbourne, and 45,000 at Sydney. Such great crowds have their effect on most players, and increase the tension, particularly on those occasions when the fans take exception to the tactics of a player. If you do not put up a good performance in Sydney, for instance, you are in trouble right away, although most of the barracking which comes from the Hill is extremely humorous, and certainly not meant to be offensive.

I think the funniest remark I ever heard at Sydney was hurled at Trevor Bailey. Trevor was playing one of his typical defensive innings, and looked like staying at the wicket for a long time without making many runs. Suddenly a wag on the Hill shouted :

" You've been there so long, Bailey, that it's time they sent you back to the Old Bailey ! "

From Tasmania we returned to the mainland for a match against a South Australian Country XI at Renmark. I have reason to remember that game vividly—and with painful memories, too.

We were fielding, and Denis Compton bowled a " Chinaman ", dropping it a bit short. The batsman stepped back and swung round to crack the ball to the boundary. He hit the ball all right, but he swung round so far that he struck me right between the eyes ! I had to go to hospital to have a couple of stitches in the gash, and I still have the scar where that bat " hit me for six " !

Naturally, I could not carry on behind the wicket because of the blood and congestion over the eye, but the Country XI captain allowed Arthur McIntyre to take over the gloves for the rest of the innings. Believe me, I shall not forget Renmark as long as I live. Every time I look into the mirror I remember it !

After beating South Australia at Adelaide, we prepared for the fourth Test. Having lost the first three, we wondered if our fortunes would change on that Adelaide wicket which is usually so good. We were not left wondering for long.

Freddie Brown lost the toss yet again and Australia took first knock on a perfect wicket. Our great hope was Alec Bedser. Alec had already bowled Arthur Morris four times in the last five Test innings, and we were quite sure

he could do it again.   But this time the " hoodoo " did
not work.   Arthur Morris found all his old form, as he
did in 1946 where he got 100 in each innings.   For the
first 70 runs he was right out of touch, he just couldn't
find his form, yet the wicket was so good that the ball
kept hitting the middle of his bat.   Then all of a sudden
he clicked, and from then on he played beautifully and
made 206.   It was a really great innings.

Australia got on top, but then Len Hutton came back
with a fighting 156.   I remember it so well, for it was the
highlight of our first innings.   Len became the first
English opening batsman for a very long time to carry
his bat right through an innings.   Nor shall I ever forget
Keith Miller's dismissal off Doug Wright when he stood
at 99 !   He moved too late to a shortish ball, tried to
cut it and only succeeded in chopping it on to the top of
the stumps.   I remember it so well because the bail flew
off and hit me in the eye !

One other incident in that Adelaide match makes me
smile when I recall it.   In Australia's second innings,
John Warr got his first Test wicket.   If it had not been
for the kindness of Ian Johnson walking from the wicket,
the umpire would have given him " not out ", so surprised was he when I caught the ball.

John Warr is a great character and we had a lot of fun
with him during the tour, but from a bowling point of
view he was never a great success.   He wasn't quite fast
enough on those true Australian wickets.   Off the field,
however, John was in great demand, especially for his
witty after-dinner speeches.   He kept us in fits of laughter, and for that reason he was a valuable member of the
touring side.

Four down and one to play—so let us pass straight to
the fifth and final Test at Melbourne.   It brings memories
of victory I shall never forget, for it was my first taste of
blood against Australia !

Once again we lost the toss, but put Australia out for
217, thanks mainly to Alec Bedser and Freddie Brown.
When we batted, I shall always remember Reg Simpson's

magnificent innings which more than anything enabled us to achieve the elusive victory that had been avoiding our grasp for so long.

Having bowled Australia out for 217, we replied with 246 for 9. It looked like the end of our innings, but then Reg Simpson and Roy Tattersall came together. They stayed together for more than an hour and added 74 runs. Roy's score was practically negligible, but he played a great backing-up game, while Reg displayed all the shots in the book. He went dashing down the wicket to Lindwall, he square-cut Miller, he hooked, cut and drove with superb power, and when Roy was finally bowled, we led by 103.

It was due to that fine innings of Reg Simpson's that we managed to win the fifth Test, but we must not forget our bowlers when we hand out the credits.

I well remember the ball that bowled Lindsay Hassett. Doug Wright pitched it on the leg stump, it turned and Lindsay was too late as it tickled the top of the off stump. It was a magnificent ball—one of Doug's best—and a valuable wicket, for Lindsay looked like staying. Len Hutton took a couple of diving slip catches and so did Alec Bedser. Alec really had been our mainstay from the bowling point of view throughout the tour, and to see him fling himself to the right and take a magnificent slip catch made us feel real proud of him.

Anyway, we won the Test, and perhaps it was only fitting that Len Hutton should make the winning hit. What a thrill that gave us ! He had played so magnificently throughout the tour that no one begrudged this great cricketer the honour of making the winning hit. It was the first time England had beaten Australia since way back in 1936—a run of twenty-six consecutive Tests, and I cannot describe our innermost feelings when the match ended. It was victory at last, although, of course, our joy was slightly tempered by the thought that we were four-one down in the series.

Nevertheless, the partial achievement of our ambition put us all in great spirits, and, I feel sure, marked the turning point in English post-war cricket. But more of that later.

From Australia we went to New Zealand, and gained victory in one of the two Tests, the other being drawn, so I think we can say that the tour was quite a success, although not financially. However, that is hardly any real business of mine, so let me sum up the playing side of the tour.

The outstanding bowler of the tour, of course, was Alec Bedser. Throughout the series he bowled magnificently to capture a record number of wickets, and on the whole I feel he was equal to, or even better than, Maurice Tate in his prime.

With regard to the batting, as I have told you already, Len Hutton was tremendous. We started by dropping him to No. 5 for the first Test, thinking that perhaps he would be able to give the middle batting more stability. But we had to revert to Len as our No. 1 and he never once let us down.

Of the all-rounders Trevor Bailey did all that was expected of him. Reg Simpson, with that grand innings of his at Melbourne, could be said to have had a successful tour, but other than those I have mentioned, nobody really came up to standard. Denis Compton of course had a very disappointing tour, and it was a great pity to see such a fine player have such a disheartening time in the Test matches. In the State games he was top of the batting averages every time. He hit four hundreds, and always looked his old self, but he could not get going in the Tests. It was one of those unaccountable misfortunes which could happen to anyone, but poor Denis just could not seem to get over it, and, of course, the Press did not help matters with some of their rather unkind criticisms.

I do not want to be unfair to the Press, who do cricket such a power of good—we could not do without it—but I must admit that it was difficult at times not to feel a little annoyed at some of the reports we read in the Press—so often reports of misbehaviour on the part of one or other of the touring players, reports, too, with no semblance of truth in them.

I recall the incident in which Denis Compton split his eyebrow. I read all sorts of reports of how that happened —some of them not very complimentary to Denis, and after we had returned home, friends in this country told me of the rumours that went around concerning that unfortunate accident.

It is only fair to Denis to report the incident as it actually happened, for I was there. It was at a party in Melbourne, at the house of Bill and Margaret Gluth, who so kindly entertained us. Denis was demonstrating a cricket shot on the edge of the lawn, when our host came along and gave him a gentle push in the side, saying : " Go on, Denis—you don't know what you're talking about ! "

It was all done in fun, of course, but Denis was caught off balance and the sharp bone above his eyebrow grazed against the static water nozzle that was there for the purpose of watering the lawn. As a matter of fact, Denis got up, laughed and carried on his demonstration. It was not for some moments that we noticed blood showing above his eye.

I have done some boxing in my time, and I know from experience how easy it is to get a cut eyebrow, even from the lightest blow. It might amaze you to know that Denis had to have six stitches in his wound, and yet he did not feel the blow at all. I am afraid the Press made rather a splash of this incident—and the reports were very far from the truth. I was there and I saw it all. It WAS a static water nozzle, whatever anybody else has said about it. . . .

You will see from this one incident how careful players have to be whilst on tour, especially when there are thirty or forty Pressmen travelling in the party from place to place throughout the tour. These reporters do not all write the same story of any particular incident, and nothing is more likely to create the wrong impression.

Much the same is true of actual match reports, and I,

for one, take little notice of them as they are printed.   Not that ALL match reports are garbled versions of what goes on, but I have found that some players, particularly the younger ones, are inclined to worry when they do not get a good " Press ".   I have heard from Keith Miller, Arthur Morris and one or two other Australians, that they do not read reports of matches in which they are playing, and I think this is a policy that should be adopted by young players in England.   After all, a player knows well enough how he is playing, and how he fared in the match being reported, so why put himself to unnecessary worry and concern ?

I recall on that 1950–51 tour, when we were losing the Tests, how some of the Pressmen blamed the players for staying out late and going to too many parties.   How wrong they were—but what a poor impression this sort of thing must make upon those who are not there, and are not, therefore, in a position to know the truth.

It is a pity that these things happen, for the Press can do so much good for cricket, and I am quite certain that the majority of Pressmen have only the good of cricket at heart.   But one false report or one garbled story of a minor incident, can do so much harm to the greatest game in the world.

Sorry to have gone off on such a tangent, but it was something about which I feel so strongly that I wanted to get it off my chest.   However, back to the players who did so gallantly on that tour.

Freddie Brown, as captain, was really magnificent throughout.   Despite the lack of success of the team, from the playing point of view, and possibly from the financial angle, too, and not having a tremendous side with him, he really pulled his weight in every direction, and we were very proud of him.

When he left England, many people contended that he would not score many runs, for he was supposed to be too susceptible to fast bowling, but he was always in the runs —and among the wickets, too.   In the last Test at Melbourne, he bowled nearly all day and fielded brilliantly,

Freddie Brown leads the 1950–51 team on to the field for a Country match at Renmark (W. Australia). You can see how much it resembles an English County ground, with the boys squatting on the grass with their bottles of pop, and the girls with their cameras.

Len Hutton introduces the author to Her Majesty the Queen at Lord's, during the second Test match against India. The late Mr. Donald Finlay, President of the M.C.C. at the time, is on the left. Other players are Alec Bedser and Roly Jenkins.

Godfrey Evans has many outside interests, not the least of which is motoring. Here he is one of the panel of judges at the Aston Martin Owners' Club Rally, held at Thame (Oxfordshire). The author is a member of the club.

and on several other occasions it was Freddie's inspiring leadership that pulled us out of the mire.

Brian Close, the youngest member of the side, was rather disappointing. He had every chance to enjoy a successful tour, but never really came off. As sometimes happens with young players, lack of big-match experience was a handicap to him. The young player often thinks he knows how to play before he has gained enough experience to show him that he still has much to learn, and when he comes up against tough opposition, and has a bit of a bad run, he is not fully equipped to face up to it. Often, too, this young player, quite naturally, I suppose, does not take sufficient notice of the advice given him by older colleagues. In consequence, he fails.

I hate to criticise, but I think this is what really happened to Brian. Yet I am sure that his experiences on this tour did him untold good, and if he gets a chance to go on tour again with the M.C.C.—as I am certain he will —we shall see a very different Brian. He certainly has it in him to succeed. He has wonderful anticipation in the field ; he has a very fine pair of hands for catching ; is a very useful bowler—he can bowl either quickish stuff off the seam, or accurate off-spinners, for he tries to spin the ball—and does. Finally, his left-hand batting, once he gets going, is really delightful to watch. He reminds one of Frank Woolley, because he is not frightened to hit the ball in the air.

After all, if you are hitting the ball in the air, although you are taking chances, you usually hit it *over* the fielders, which means runs. Frank Woolley's policy, when he was playing, was to get on top of the bowling and stay on top, and once Brian Close gets going, he certainly does just that. He proved it in Perth where he got a hundred. He really was hitting the ball wonderfully well that day.

Of the rest of the team, John Dewes was not particularly outstanding, although he was somewhat unfortunate. He was not at all well during the second Test, otherwise we might have pulled that off.

Johnny Warr, as I have told you, was not a great

3

success. His bowling pace was not quite quick enough for Australia ; he does not do enough with the ball. His fielding, too, was hardly of Test standard. I recall one incident in Brisbane—I am sure he will remember it, too. He went to catch the ball but was so perturbed that the ball was coming his way, that he tried to push it away before he was in position to catch it. The batsman should have been out for single figures, but instead, went on to make a hundred. However, Johnny was a great character and certainly kept us in high spirits.

Gilbert Parkhouse proved himself a cricketer of considerable ability, although his few chances early on in the tour seemed to upset him, and he did not really come off as he had done in the previous season in England, where he looked absolutely in the top class as a batsman. He was a fine fielder close to the wicket, but I am sure it was because of his lack of playing chances that he did not show up as well as was expected.

David Sheppard played a very good knock in the fourth Test but on the whole had rather a disappointing tour.

Eric Hollies and Bob Berry, those two excellent chums, who were such great friends throughout the tour, both just missed being in the top class. Their flight and trajectory seemed to allow the ball to drop a little short and thus give the batsmen time to get right back and crack them to mid-wicket, which the Australians are so very fond of doing. In short, they did not really capture the correct way of bowling on those very hard wickets and with the atmosphere so bright, but they were excellent companions to all of us. When they were not playing they were always willing to help the rest of us in a dozen and one ways. Yes, they were grand fellows !

Douglas Wright, of course, was not the force he was in 1946, but he bowled well at times, and with a little more support from the fielding, I think he might have had a much more successful tour.

Roy Tattersall and Brian Statham were flown out to join us during the tour, but I do not think the results justified it. Brian was rather disappointing, but what could one expect of a man coming from England's snow directly into the heat of Adelaide, where the temperature was over 100 when he had to bowl? Considering that he was playing within six days of arriving from icy cold to that intense heat, with no practice—well, he did jolly well, and I am sure the experience he gained helped him to develop into the wonderfully accurate pace-man he is today.

So much for the 1950–51 tour. It was not too successful, although we did win that final Test, but, as I have said, it was to prove the turning point in England's Test fortunes—as the future showed.

CHAPTER III

South Africa, 1951—Dudley Nourse's Men

THE CHAPTERS OF ENGLAND'S TEST STORY AGAINST SOUTH Africa make most interesting reading, for the men from the Union have always played cricket in the finest spirit. In five Test series against them since the war, I have had some enjoyable experiences, yet, somehow, I have always been a bit unlucky against South Africa. Don't ask me why. It is just one of those unaccountable things that happen, and no fault attaches to the South Africans.

One thing we can thank them for—they usually bring good weather with them ! I remember that 1947 was a magnificent season so far as the weather was concerned. South Africa were also very lucky with the weather and the result of the Test series during their last trip here, for 1955 was one of the finest summers for many years, and the South African tour was most successful from the financial angle. However, at the moment I want to deal briefly with the 1951 season.

The South Africans were a fine side, although it was regrettable that we were seeing some of them for the last time as cricket tourists. Among these great characters was their captain, Dudley Nourse, a very sound, solid player, who had been the backbone of South African cricket for many years, long before the war even. His father, too, was a magnificent cricketer and also captained South Africa. Then there was Eric Rowan, the vice-captain, out on his own as a cricketer. He was an unmistakable personality, although everybody did not agree with his policy. I understand that on several occasions he annoyed the South African Board of Control because of his manner on the field. But it takes courage —a lot of courage—to be a really great cricketer and an outstanding personality, and Eric Rowan was certainly that. He was a man with ideas and the pluck to play according to his convictions.

He told me of an incident that happened when Australia visited South Africa. In one match Ray Lindwall had been bowling a profusion of bouncers and then, whilst Eric was batting, Lindwall sent down a particularly fast bumper that whistled past Eric's ear. Eric glared down the pitch at the Australian pace-man and said :

" What's the matter with you ? I thought you were supposed to be quick ! "

When play was resumed after lunch Eric went out to face Ray again—without any batting gloves !

Call it bravado, if you will, but one has to admire a man who treats his cricket in that way. Eric was no " show-off ", and he certainly proved in this country that he could do an outstanding job when it was necessary— and do it well. At Leeds, for instance, he was at the wicket for over 9 hours and hit 236, the highest score for a South African in a Test match in England.

I was not playing in the match. I was out of form with the bat and behind the stumps, and Don Brennan took my place. I remember Don telling me on a later occasion how Eric had squatted on the pitch when the Leeds crowd objected to his slow scoring, and refused to continue until the slow hand-clapping had stopped.

Eric was criticised for his action, but I am quite sure that accusations of his bad sportsmanship were quite unwarranted. At heart he is a really sound chap indeed. He has done a heap of good for cricket, particularly in his encouragement of South Africa's youngsters, and I feel that his disappearance from Test cricket was most regrettable.

Few of us who admired the bowling of " Tufty " Mann —as we all knew him—realised that we were watching him for the last time. You may remember that soon after his return to South Africa he passed away after an operation. All the England players and, I am certain, all other cricketers who ever played with or against

Tufty, knew him as a grand chap, a first-rate sportsman, and a fine left-arm slow bowler.

Another of the outstanding players of that 1951 tour was Cuan McCarthy, the young fast bowler. I first saw him when he was 17 years old, and he looked a great prospect to me. He was fast—and I really mean fast—and I once heard Len Hutton say : " I think Cuan McCarthy is even faster than Lindwall and Miller." Coming from such a great player as Len, that was praise indeed. But McCarthy missed real greatness because I think he was over-bowled during the earlier stages in his career, and then, when he reached Test status, he bowled too many short balls. Batsmen got used to his short bouncer and merely ducked out of its way. In consequence, Cuan did not get the wickets he should have done.

The bouncer must be used sparingly, varied with the slower and the faster deliveries, as Ray Lindwall and Brian Statham use it, so that the batsman is kept in suspense, not knowing when a bouncer is coming. But if the bowler continually drops them short, the batsman usually gets on top, and the bouncer loses all its menace.

To return to that South African team—their leading wicket-taker was that big-hearted, untiring toiler, be-spectacled Geoff Chubb. A most cheerful soul, and a respected cricketer, he was given a lot of work to do on the tour, but showed up extremely well. Despite his lengthy run, he was not really fast—about Alec Bedser's pace—but he bowled more overs than anyone else during the tour. I played against Geoff in South Africa and he looked then just an ordinary up-and-downer, but over here, in our damper English atmosphere, he made the ball swing and proved quite a problem to many of our batsmen.

Another of the successes of that 1951 side was off-spinner Athol Rowan, making his last visit here, but he proved that he had lost little of his earlier skill. He varied his flight and direction with bewildering skill, and his pace, too. That ball of his that dropped just a shade quicker than normal and spun a little more, was a beauty. Batsmen either mishit it and were caught at short leg, or hit over the top of it as it turned away and were stumped.

To my mind, Athol was the best off-spinner in the world until his young fellow South African, Hughie Tayfield, stepped in to take over his role. Hughie Tayfield, about whom I shall have more to say later on, did not play in a Test during 1951. When we first played against him, he appeared a little green, but all the South Africans were agreed that : " This boy will be a great off-spinner." Their prediction has been fully borne out.

We needed no introduction to Clive Van Ryneveld. An Oxford double-Blue, we knew him well as a cricketer and as an international Rugger player. I saw him play at Twickenham, and admired the beautiful way he moved. If you saw him chasing the ball in the cricket outfield, you realised that he was a sportsman above the average, and if only he could have continued his cricket career he might have become one of South Africa's " great ". Rather tall in build, he flighted his leg-spinners very slowly through the air, but occasionally he turned one a little more than expected, had the batsman out of his ground and, in consequence, the wicket-keeper was given a chance.

Of the other members of that 1951 side who were eventually to make up the next South African Test team, I must include a mention of Jack Cheetham, who had a very successful season, and looked certain to become the future captain of the side. I liked the promise of wicket-keeper John Waite, too. When I first saw him in South Africa he was mainly a run-getter and kept wicket only on odd occasions, but over here he found plenty to do as stumper as well as run-getter, and he certainly did a very efficient job.

At the completion of that 1951 tour I made some notes for future reference and looking them up recently I see I wrote of John Waite : " Should become a really great 'keeper. One to watch for the future."

I made a note, too, of Jackie McGlew—" Sticker " we

call him, because he never gives his wicket away without
a fight. " He is only quite young, very keen, very fit, and
always on his toes in the field. His enthusiasm is inspiring
and I am sure that one day he will come back to England
and do extraordinarily well."

Of Roy McLean I wrote : " The best stroke-maker
among the younger brigade. He plays all the shots in
the game, and is wonderfully good in the outfield, possibly
one of the best the South Africans have had for years. . . .
I am certain that these young men will form the nucleus
of future South African teams that will eventually give
us a lot of Test trouble. . . ."

However, that is enough of my opinions, so let us now
take a brief glance at the 1951 Tests.

At Trent Bridge, the Springboks started off like a
bomb. They won the toss and, naturally, put us into the
field. It was a typical Nottingham wicket, and even
Alec Bedser failed to get much help from it. The South
Africans really got on top, and Dudley Nourse played a
magnificent innings, although that is an understatement.
He was eventually run out after scoring 208—yet throughout the whole of that epic innings, lasting 9¼ hours,
Dudley played with a broken thumb, which was pinned
up with metal in a fantastic sort of way. Fortunately, it
was on the right hand and, therefore, he could hold the
bat firmly with the left hand, but every shot must have
given him excruciating pain, for the longer he stayed at
the wicket, the more the thumb swelled. It was one of
the pluckiest innings I have ever seen and I am sure it
was Dudley's magnificent performance with the bat that
gave South Africa a chance of victory.

Anyway, it was a good performance on their part to
score 483, for we had a strong attack, with Bedser at his
best ; Freddie Brown bowling his leg-spinners and sometimes the odd seamer ; Roy Tattersall with his off-spinners, and Johnny Wardle.

When it was our turn to bat on that wonderful Nottingham wicket, we started badly. John Ikin got a nasty one
from Geoff Chubb, who was bowling very well at the time,

and was caught by McCarthy at second gulley. Then we settled down. Len Hutton hit 63, Reg Simpson 137, Denis Compton 112 and Willie Watson 57, and it looked as though we should pass South Africa's total, but it was not to be. Geoff Chubb and Cuan McCarthy got four wickets a-piece in the innings, and when Freddie Brown declared with 9 wickets down, we were more than 60 runs short.

Well, as so often happens during a five-day Test, we had some rain. A shower of this nature is always helpful to the bowlers, and this again proved the case. Alec took full advantage of the changed conditions and in South Africa's second innings took 6 for 37. It was Alec at his best, and he and Roy Tattersall between them put them out (minus Skipper Nourse, of course) for 121.

It looked as though we still had a chance, but we underestimated the capabilities of Athol Rowan and Tufty Mann, who bowled almost unchanged throughout the innings. These two plugged away manfully on this wicket which now was definitely giving them a lot of help, causing the batsmen to struggle for runs. A great contest ended with South Africa winning by a margin of 71. It gave South Africa a tremendous uplift, because before the series started it was thought that England's chances of winning the rubber were considerable. However, fortunes were to change before the end of the series.

As always, Lord's staged the second Test—Lord's with all its tradition. There is no ground in the country with the same atmosphere. To me it is always an inspiration to play on this historic wicket.

This particular Test against South Africa will always be known as Tattersall's Match. The Lancashire off-spinner could do nothing wrong. He was in great form with the ball after Freddie Brown had won the toss and we had scored 311, thanks to Denis Compton and Willie Watson. Each scored 79, and even Alec Bedser came into his own towards the end with 26 not out.

Then came rain ! At Nottingham it was to our dis-advantage—at Lord's the fortunes were reversed, for a storm on the second day turned the pitch into a spinner's paradise. In consequence, Roy Tattersall was very nearly unplayable. Take a look at his analysis : he bowled 28 overs (10 of them maidens) for 52 runs and 7 wickets, with Johnny Wardle holding the fort at the opposite end and taking the other three wickets.

However, I know that Roy would be the first to admit that he owed a great deal to some excellent close-to-the-wicket catching. Ikin took a couple of beauties and Freddie Brown held a very fine catch to dismiss Tufty Mann. First-class close-to-the-wicket fielders like John Ikin and one or two others, are a great asset to a bowler of Tattersall's flight and spin.

South Africa fared a little better in their second innings, but Roy again got among their wickets. I remember, however, a grand knock by Jack Cheetham, who scored 54 although suffering from a stiff neck which made batting decidedly difficult. Brian Statham eventually bowled him with a beauty. I can see that middle stump now flying out of the ground to put a virtual end to South Africa's only real resistance. We needed a mere 16 runs to finish the game, and won by 10 wickets.

This Lord's Test was made memorable for me because during the tea interval on the Friday we were introduced to Princess Elizabeth, a proud honour for the players of both teams. I have now had the great privilege of meeting all the members of the Royal Family, and I never cease to admire the natural charm and the easy manner which they bring to such official functions.

From Lord's we moved to Old Trafford, which has been a fairly lucky ground for England. I cannot remember us losing many Tests in Manchester, at least not since I have been playing Test cricket—although I am not taking the credit for that ! So we were favourites for the Old Trafford match, and the favourites won by 9 wickets.

As usual the Manchester weather lived up to its doubtful reputation, and there was rain about during the whole of the match, but I do not think this helped our side to any marked degree. However, it may be that we were fortunate in losing the toss, for Dudley Nourse elected to bat and this gave Alec Bedser a decided advantage. It was a wicket after his own heart, and he was able to move the ball about as only he can. With rain about, and moisture on the turf, the ball retains its shine so much longer, and this combination of conditions allows Alec to use the ball in a most disconcerting way even after he has been bowling for considerable periods.

During his opening overs I remember he bowled a couple of perfect in-swingers and then an away-spinner, and South Africa had lost two most vital wickets. It was an inspiring start and we knew we had a good chance of putting the South Africans out cheaply. As a matter of fact we did, and it was only a stubborn partnership by Clive Van Ryneveld and Dudley Nourse that gave them a fighting chance, but we eventually had them all back in the pavilion for 158.

When we batted, it soon became obvious that we were not to get it all our own way, for Geoff Chubb was able to do much the same as Alec. He kept the ball swinging about, and worried most of the England batsmen. He fully deserved his six wickets by his consistency throughout the whole innings, which realised only 211. The South African fielding was of a high standard, but perhaps the best work was done by John Waite behind the stumps. He put up a great performance, conceding only four byes and stumping Reg Simpson off Tufty Mann and catching me off Geoff Chubb.

In South Africa's second innings Alec Bedser again bowled superbly, and so did his Surrey colleague, off-spinner Jim Laker. Jim is a good bowler on any type of wicket but particularly when it offers help to the spinners, as this one did, for he really does flick that ball. I have often heard it buzzing down the wicket even from my position behind the stumps—most disconcerting, for the 'keeper never knows just how much it is going to turn. But neither does the batsman !

Alec Bedser finished the tail off in 5 overs, taking 5 wickets for 11 runs, making 12 wickets in all in the match.

We were left with 139 to get to win, and after a fighting
display by Len and Jack Ikin, following a hold-up for rain,
the odds were on them finishing it off before lunch on the
final day.   Len was in full command, and it was obvious
that he was determined to get his 100—his hundredth in
first-class cricket.

Len's wish to achieve this wonderful milestone in his
career was understandable, and we were all as keen as he
was to see him do it, BUT . . . ominous clouds were
gathering, and the thing that mattered most was that we
scored the necessary runs for victory.   If both could be
achieved before the rain came, and coming it was, then
everything would be all right, but some of us began to
have doubts. . . .

When Jack Ikin was bowled, Reg Simpson joined Len,
and a good many runs were still needed.   It was more
obvious than ever now that if the runs were not on the
board by lunch-time, the threatening rain might blot out
the remainder of the game.   Yet those runs were not
coming as fast as most of us would have liked.

Len did his best to collar the bowling, and his own score
mounted steadily, but Reg Simpson's only thought seemed
to be to give Len the bowling.   There were fours waiting
to be hit, but Reg preferred to take singles, so that Len
could have the bowling.   We could appreciate Reg's
spirit, but as I watched I felt he was playing entirely the
wrong game.   I am sure most cricketers would agree that
when runs are needed to win a match, personal interests
should not be considered.

In this particular instance, even if Len had reached 99
and 10 runs were still needed to win the match, then Reg
Simpson should have made every effort to score those runs
as quickly as possible, in view of the impending rain.

Then, just before lunch, down came the rain—and still
the match had not been won.   I must admit that at this
stage, my concern was becoming a little personal.   You
see, I had a ticket for the Randolph Turpin-Sugar Ray
Robinson world title fight at Harringay that evening, and
I was anxious to get away as soon as I could to drive to

London.   However, keeping my fingers crossed, I packed my bags during the lunch interval and waited. . . .

Fortunately for all concerned, the rain ceased long enough for play to continue soon after lunch.   A few balls finished it—but Len did not get his hundred.   I remember it so well.   He hit a " two " and a single off Cuan McCarthy's first over, and then faced Norman Mann, wanting six for his century, although four would win the match for us.

Hoping to achieve both with one hit, Len clouted Mann high over cover.   It looked a six all the way, but it dropped just short of the boundary.   We had won the Test, but Len had missed his hundredth hundred by a mere two runs.

Naturally, we were sorry that he had not achieved his ambition in a Test match, but, fortunately, he reached his coveted objective a few days later, in a County game.

After that game, my lean time with the bat and behind the stumps continued, and I was not really surprised when I was dropped for the fourth Test at Leeds.

Don Brennan of Yorkshire was selected to keep wicket, an excellent choice, for he was just about the best stumper in the country.   What a pity he had to give up first-class cricket because of his business commitments.

That fourth Test at Leeds was notable for the wonderful innings of 236 by Eric Rowan, a really brilliant performance in the circumstances.   He was missed a couple of times but other than that he played a magnificent innings.   A pity some of the spectators gave him the slow hand-clap.   They seemed to forget that South Africa were one down in the series and their obvious intention was to try to get a commanding lead, because with the Leeds wicket being one of the best in the country, and with rain always likely, they might at least stave off defeat.   They certainly achieved their object, for they managed to collect a total of 538, which put them in a very sound position.

In reply, England also made good use of that perfect wicket.   In our total of 505 were a couple of centuries—

one by Len Hutton, and the other by Peter May. Peter played a magnificent innings of 138 and was hailed as a future world star. We must not forget Trevor Bailey either. Always a most reliable standby when things are going wrong, Trevor scored just five runs short of his hundred, a valiant effort when you recall that he was suffering from a badly strained back.

After rain had curtailed play, the match ended in a draw with South Africa just playing out time. It was a shame that the game could not be finished, but on such a good batting wicket this was not really surprising.

So South Africa went to the Oval one-down and with only one match to play.

To save the rubber they had to win. A drawn match would not suit them. However, as it happened, England won by four wickets.

I was up on the balcony watching some of the game, and judging from the run of the play, it could easily have been South Africa's match.

Few reputations were made or enhanced, although Jim Laker, on his home ground, bowled extremely well and finished with four wickets in the first innings and six in the second. Jim proved once again that he is a more than useful bowler under most conditions. Alec Bedser was not quite his usual dominating self, and the English fielding, I thought, seemed a bit lackadaisical. It was not one of their best games.

Freddie Brown lost the toss—(the twelfth time he had lost it in 15 Tests)—and South Africa had a great chance. Russell Endean was brought in as opener in place of John Waite, who was injured, and he and Eric Rowan gave the side a good start.

Russell Endean, who has a very limited back lift, had not had a very good season in England, but nevertheless, he was always a difficult chap to get out.

The visitors were 66 for 1 when Russell was eventually caught by Freddie Brown off Jim Laker. He went out to drive, did not quite get hold of it, and Freddie made the catch. From then on we were on top and it was only a fighting innings by Athol Rowan that enabled South Africa to push their score past the 200 mark.

Things looked bright for England. 200 did not seem much of a total, but as we have seen on so many occasions in Test matches, 200 on the board is better than 200 in theory. So much can happen to spoil the brightest prospect.

Well, England were up against it right from the start, for the first wicket went with only 2 runs on the board. Showers put life into the pitch and South Africa bowled us out for 194.

Now it was up to our bowlers, and they responded valiantly, sending the South Africans back for 154. This meant that England needed 163 to win, and Yorkshire's opening partners gave the side a good start with a 53 stand in fairly awkward conditions. Then Len Hutton was out in a rather amazing way.

He went to hit one round to leg, but the ball flew off the top edge of the bat, bounced high and began to drop right over the top of the wicket. Len acted instinctively, raised his bat and deflected the ball from the wicket. Now there is nothing wrong with a batsman stopping the ball from hitting his wicket, but in this case, Russell Endean, the wicket-keeper, was just about to take the ball, and Len's action prevented the catch being made. According to the Laws, this is " obstructing the field "— and Len was given out by Umpire Dai Davies.

It was an unfortunate ending to Len's 100th Test innings, but I feel that Russell Endean had good reason to appeal, and the umpire's decision was quite fair, although, of course, the incident was a controversial subject for days afterwards.

After Len had gone, wickets fell quickly. Four were down for 90 and it looked as if South Africa really had a chance, for the ball was beginning to do some quite extraordinary things. However, Freddie Brown took over— he always did love a situation of that sort. Anyway, he started hitting the ball all over the field, and in next to no time he had scored 40. He was bowled just before the finish, but England won that final Test with four wickets to spare. The whole match was as close as the finish, and it might have gone either way towards the end. However, it was not South Africa's day and England had won the rubber by 3–1.

1951 was not one of my happiest seasons—no cricketer enjoys being out of form, whatever the cause. But towards the end of the season the outlook grew very much brighter. After hitting 52 against Gloucester at Dover, Kent went to Leicester for our final match, and I had the pleasure of hitting the first 100 I had ever scored for my County.

Our skipper, Bill Murray Wood, won the toss and asked my advice. He was doubtful about the wicket for rain had seeped under the cover, but as there was a likelihood of more rain over the week-end when the wicket would not be covered, I suggested that we should bat. Arthur Fagg agreed, although, in his whimsical way he added : " We shall be about 20 for 5 ! "

Arthur was not far wrong, in fact, we *were* at one time about 20 for 5. Wooler, a Southern Rhodesian, bowling quite quickish, took the 5 wickets for 13. It was not the state of the wicket that caused the collapse, however, but sheer bad batting, playing across the line of the ball and lack of concentration. Anyway, with the score at 20 for 5, I went in to bat, hoping against hope that I could make some runs. Well, my luck was in and I seemed to find my form right from the word " go ".

Wickets continued to tumble at the other end, but I was still collecting a few runs. When Fred Ridgway, our last man, came in, I was in the sixties and I thought our only chance of getting a few more runs was for me to pinch the bowling as much as possible. But Fred had other ideas. As he reached the wicket he said :

" Play your own game, Godfrey. Try and get the bowling if you can, but don't worry if you can't. I will stop and block up this end."

Between us we managed quite well and added 63 runs for the last wicket. Fred scored 8 not out and I reached

The author's three homes, which he mentions in this book—(*top*) Lords, at Sheldwich, near Faversham ; (*centre*) The Wickets, at Bearsted ; and Wild Acre, at Aylesford

Godfrey Evans in a serious mood with Peter Ustinov, at the Savoy Hotel,
on the occasion of the author's election to honorary membership of the
Lord's Taverners.

Having dropped Neil Harvey from a relatively easy chance when his score
was only 3, the author made amends with this more difficult leg-side
catch off Alec Bedser to dismiss the Australian left-hander—after he had
scored 122. (Manchester 1953.)

my first 100 for Kent—caught on the boundary for 101. It was a most encouraging finish to the season for me, following a disheartening spell.

On reflection I am convinced that my loss of form, resulting in my deposition from the Test team, was the result of too much cricket. Playing six days a week throughout a long English season and then winter tours as well, is a great mental as well as physical strain on any player. In my case I had had only one winter's rest since the war and I was definitely feeling jaded. Fortunately, following that summer of 1951 I was due for another winter's rest, and I can assure you I was ready for it.

The benefit I derived from that winter's lay-off was fully evident during the next English season. . . .

4

India in England, 1952—My Finest Season

INDIA WILL ALWAYS HOLD A PROMINENT PLACE IN MY memories, for I made my Test debut against India in 1946. It was the last match of the series, at the Oval. I did not travel to India with the M.C.C. party in 1951, however, so it was not until the summer of 1952 that I again had the pleasure of meeting the Indians. But before I describe the highlights of that Test series, I want to deal at some length with the 1952 season.

It was a very memorable summer for me—one of the best of my whole career, speaking personally, of course. Memories of that season crowd in upon me—a Test century—the second of my career—that nearly became a record " 100-before-lunch " ; my 100 Test victims in that same match ; a memorable meeting with Her Majesty the Queen, at Lord's ; and my personal record of 1,500 runs with the bat during the season, which was the subject of a much-publicised wager.

Tom Crawford, a very well-known Kent C.C.C. member, and himself a very good cricketer, bet me 20 to 1 that I would not score 1,500 runs during the season. Being—I hope—a sportsman, I took him on, in fivers, and the luck was on my side.

I shall never forget the day I reached my £100 total of 1,500. It was against Essex at Clacton. Very nice spot, Clacton ! We had a pleasant week-end by the sea and then, on the last day, I needed exactly 31 runs to reach my 1,500. After several " heart attacks ", I took my total to 30. Off the new ball I had a mighty crack. It was fielded at cover but went through for two. That was my 32. I was there !

Next ball from Ray Smith I had another crack, but this time Bill Greensmith caught me at extra cover. It was a grand catch for he jumped high, knocked the ball up and caught it on the rebound. However, I had hit my target of 1,500 and you can be sure I was very delighted. But what really mattered was that my 32 helped us to beat Essex—with only four minutes to spare. That's cricket as I like it—and as the crowd enjoy it.

I hope no one viewed my friendly bet with Tom Crawford in the wrong light. I appreciate that it would be easy to do so, especially as I reached my target and won the wager. You might have thought that I was given unfair advantages—that I was allowed to bat on at times when we did not really need the extra runs—or was given chances to bat high up in the list in preference to established batsmen. I assure you that nothing of that sort happened. I hope I am too good a sportsman to be a party to anything that was not in the best interests of my side.

Tom Crawford was adamant when he made the bet that I should go for my runs fairly and squarely.

" I would not dream of entertaining you, Godfrey," he said, " if I thought you were at any time playing for yourself—and for the money—rather than for your side."

Well, so much for the 1,500 runs bet, although why my batting was so much better that season than ever before, I cannot tell you. Right from the start, however, I felt I was going to have a good season. I seemed to have found a new concentration and confidence in my batting. Every time I picked up a bat, I felt like " having a go ". Maybe it was my *lucky* season, too, for everything seemed to go right.

I remember I hit 137 at Bristol against Gloucestershire, and did not waste much time in getting them.

I had another wonderful day with the bat against Somerset at Taunton, where I hit my highest score in first-class cricket—144 in 110 minutes. I was going in No. 3 in those days—obviously the captain had faith in me ! So as soon as Arthur Fagg was out early on, I took his place at the wicket. I was 80 not out at lunch, which wasn't bad going. We started again at ten past two and I was back in the pavilion at half past two with my score at 144 !

My luck was certainly in that day. Somerset played right into my hands, and put on their slow bowlers, Johnny Lawrence and Ellis Robinson. This was just what the doctor ordered and I was soon jumping down the wicket and cracking them on the half volley, and when they pitched it up, I hit it straight over their heads. After I had cracked Ellis Robinson for two sixes in one over, he said to me in his broad Yorkshire dialect :

" Ee, what's going on ? What dost'a mean by doing that ? "

" Well," I grinned back, " if you bowl that trash, Ellis, you expect to get hit, don't you ? "

It was all in fun, of course, but Ellis never forgave me for that remark and he had his revenge, for he got me out in the end !

But that's enough about my batting for a time, so let's take a quick look at the 1952 Test series against the Indians.

1952 was memorable for the fact that a professional captain was chosen for the first time to lead England. It was Len Hutton, of course, and it was appropriate that he, a Yorkshireman, was selected for the first Test at Leeds. We all thought it an excellent choice, and in wishing him luck, we expressed the hope that he would continue as England's captain for many Tests to come. Our hopes were fulfilled. . . .

That first Test, at Leeds, also saw the debut of a young fast bowler—Freddie Trueman. He took the chance with real Yorkshire grit, and it was obvious that he was a trump card for the future. Throughout the series, Freddie did very well, although I feel that the opposition was not really up to the normal Test match standard. Not that the Indians were a poor side, but they cracked too easily against the power of our pace attack, which seemed to unsettle the majority of their batsmen.

In that first Test at Leeds, which opened in quite good batting conditions, only Hazare, the skipper, and young Manjrekar offered any real resistance. These two were always difficult to dislodge throughout the series, but on the whole, the others had no real answer to our pace bowling, particularly of Freddie Trueman.

We were somewhat surprised at Polly Umrigar, whom Tom Graveney had told us was a most fluent player, and a very sound bat. Unfortunately, he failed to produce his best form in the Test series, although, strangely enough, he was one of India's outstanding batsmen in the other matches throughout the tour.

Anyway, so far as that first Test innings at Leeds was concerned, apart from Hazare and Manjrekar, who hit a fine 133, the Indian batting collapsed against the bowling of Alec Bedser, Freddie Trueman and Jim Laker.

When we had to bat in the Test at Leeds, we found ourselves on a rain-affected wicket. India should have clinched the match, even though their first innings total wasn't exactly tremendous, but on that bad wicket, perfect batting by Compton and Graveney gave us a fair start. Alan Watkins was in grand form, too. But India did not produce the fighting cricket we had expected of them, and they let slip chances that should have been snapped up.

For instance, on the Saturday morning we were in a none too happy position when it came my turn to bat. I remember Len Hutton calling to me as I went out :

" Get fifty, Godfrey, and I'll give you half a bottle of champagne."

" Right, Skipper," I said promptly enough. " You're on ! "

In such circumstances my defence is always to attack, and attack I did. I finished with 66 and with Roly Jenkins trying to outdo me with his light-hearted hitting, we managed to gain a lead of 41. Not a big lead, maybe, but it seemed completely to demoralise the Indians, because when they batted again, wickets simply tumbled.

What a sensation—and a record, too ! After 14 balls the scoreboard read " o runs for 4 wickets "—three to Freddie Trueman and one to Alec Bedser. These two fine pace bowlers, helped by Roly Jenkins, polished off the innings.

Roly is a favourite bowler of mine, being a leg-spinner, and I always enjoy 'keeping to these chaps, because they offer the 'keeper the odd stumping chance as well as a few catches.

I remember stumping Ramchand in that second innings. He dashed down the wicket to one of Roly's flighty spinners but failed to get to the pitch of it. The ball turned, came through to me and I whipped off the bails while Ramchand was still yards out of his ground.

India fought hard at Leeds, but we won by 7 wickets. Only ten days later we were due to meet again, this time at Lord's. The tourists had not really been impressive in their previous matches. It must be admitted that the weather had not been too kind to them, but, in actual fact, they were not quite strong enough. In view of this it came as no surprise to any of us when we heard that the Indians had called upon one of their countrymen who was playing for Haslingden in the Lancashire League—Vinoo Mankad, of course.

His inclusion in the team for the Lord's Test was a master stroke. He did a wonderful job—in fact, it was " Mankad's Match ".

He hit 72 in the first innings and 184 in the second. But that was not all. In between these two magnificent knocks, he showed what a superb all-rounder he was by bowling practically throughout the whole of our innings, 73 overs in all, taking 5 for 196. Wonderful !

At the completion of that marathon bowling performance, he came out to open the second innings for India. As he took his place at the wicket, I said to him :

"You must be feeling very tired."

"Yes, I am rather," he replied. "But I am going to take a chance. If it comes off—all right, but if it does not, well I shall not worry. I think I have done my bit."

As a matter of fact, he batted even better than in the first innings, showing little respect for any of our bowlers, and went on to make 184, in 4½ hours. It was magnificent, and I say it was "Mankad's Match", no question about it.

This Lord's match was a highlight in my career because I almost scored 100 before lunch, and that is something that no English Test batsman has ever done.

The crucial incident in that innings caused a great deal of discussion, especially in the Press. Many critics thought I was "robbed" of a record, but let me try to be fair about the whole business and say quite definitely that I do not agree with any of the criticisms.

Although I knew I was moving well on to my century, for Tom Graveney at the other end was playing a wonderfully unselfish game by giving me as much of the bowling as he could, when I took a quick single that took me to 98, I was not aware of the score. My only thought was for the lunch interval. I was keen to be out in the middle again when play restarted, and the scoring of a century before lunch did not really enter my head. I certainly did not realise that it would have been a record had I achieved this performance.

Anyway, the last ball of the over which I thought would be the last but one before lunch, I pushed to mid-off. Tom and I scampered a quick single, which would have given me the bowling again. As the Indians started changing over, the clock showed two minutes to 1.30, but they did not appear to hurry, and I could hardly blame them. They had been run off their feet that morning, for we had scored something like 140 in the two hours' play, and they must have been feeling the strain. At any rate, Skipper Hazare, who was to bowl that last over, took his time about rearranging his field, and then, just as he was about to make his run-up, Umpire Frank Chester lifted the bails and said :

"Time, gentlemen, please ! "

Off back to the pavilion we trooped, and personally I was glad of the respite, and delighted, too, that Tom and I were not out. Then, when I entered the pavilion and heard that I would have been the first Englishman to score a hundred before lunch in a Test match, of course I was disappointed. Wouldn't you have been ? But when some of the players and most of the spectators who spoke to me expressed the opinion that they thought Frank Chester was to blame for not allowing that last over to be bowled, I could not agree with them.

It must have been a difficult decision for Frank to make, for no doubt he knew the position of the score, but I am quite content to believe that the decision he took was the right one. If he had any reason to think that the Indians were deliberately delaying the start of that over, he would have demanded that the over be bowled. An umpire has that jurisdiction. But it was quite obvious that he did not hold that opinion, and as the clock showed less than half a minute to 1.30 before Hazare started his run-up, then he was quite right in calling a halt to the play, even though it prevented me setting up a record.

I remember Frank Chester entering the dressing-room during the luncheon interval, a gesture which I fully appreciated.

"Congratulations on a grand knock, Godfrey," he said, "but what bad luck that you could not get your hundred before lunch. If only the Indian fielders had not taken so long to position themselves, we should have had time to get in another over. But, after all, you will appreciate that it is my job, Godfrey, to come off the field at the correct time."

"That's perfectly all right, Frank," I said. "As a matter of fact, I'm more than delighted to be not out ! "

As you all know, I completed my century soon after play had resumed for the afternoon session, and incidentally, although I did not gain a record, that hundred DID bring me a reward. Before I went out to bat that morning, Len Hutton offered me a challenge.

" You got fifty in the Leeds Test, Godfrey," he said, " and I offered you half a bottle of champagne. Get a hundred this time, and I'll make it a full bottle ! "

Len was as good as his word, and the bottle of champagne was duly delivered. Perhaps I needed it after that century ! Anyway, it provided a celebration for the boys.

On the Monday of that match came another very memorable moment in my cricket life. Her Majesty the Queen and the Duke of Edinburgh paid a visit to Lord's to meet both teams. I shall never forget the moment—the brief but delightful conversation I had with Her Majesty. She congratulated me on scoring 100 runs and expressed regret that I did not get my century before lunch. She also mentioned my dismissal of a hundred Test victims. I was surprised at Her Majesty's profound knowledge of cricket, but felt very honoured that she should have singled me out for special congratulations.

So far as the rest of the match is concerned, we won by 8 wickets, despite that almost superhuman all-round performance of Vinoo Mankad, which must surely rank as one of the finest in the whole annals of Test cricket.

From Lord's we went to Old Trafford, Manchester. The Indians changed their side a bit, bringing in young wicket-keeper Pat Sen, who had done very well in his own country but had been regarded as understudy to Mantri for the first two Tests. Mantri was considered to be the better batsman, but I feel that a side should always select its *wicket-keeper* first for his skill behind the stumps.

If he can bat as well, so much the better, but if he cannot, well, he can make up for that by his wicket-keeping. It is of the utmost importance, particularly in Test cricket, that a side has its No. 1 'keeper behind the stumps, no matter whether he bats or not. But, of course, if the two wicket-keepers are equal in skill and experience behind the stumps, then the one who is the better batsman must get preference.

Manchester produced its normal weather, rain, showers, humidity and wind. India never settled down in these conditions, and one had to feel sympathy for them. However, the pitch was not too good for England's batsmen either, although with Skipper Len delighting us all with 104, we scored enough runs to get India in on that very fast wicket which had been affected by rain.

Sensations followed. We bowled India out twice in a day. I think this was the first time this had been done since 1934 when Hedley Verity bowled Australia out twice in a day at Lord's.

This time it was another Yorkshireman who did much of the damage—Freddie Trueman. Bowling from the Stretford end with a fairly strong wind behind him, he was in brilliant form, although it is only fair to say that Freddie " frightened out " the Indian batsmen.

Several times I saw batsmen moving away to square leg when Freddie was running up to bowl. On that nasty wicket, with the wind screeching down from behind the bowler, it could have been no fun for the batsmen, for Freddie was really slipping himself. Enough to scare anyone !

Well, I said just now that we bowled India out twice in one day, but really I suppose I should say " we caught them out ". Our fielding was simply brilliant and I have never seen so many fine catches held in a day's cricket. The first catch held was by Tony Lock, making his Test debut. Incidentally, it was the first time he touched the ball in Test cricket, too, and the man he caught out (for 2 off his Surrey colleague Alec Bedser) was Vinoo Mankad, who had made such a wonderful show in the Lord's Test. Tony was fielding at short-leg —today he's the best short-leg fielder in the world—and that catch was a beauty.

Another catch that deserves mention was that by David Sheppard. Phadkar hit a full-blooded sort of square slash off a very fast delivery from Trueman and David, in the gully, to protect himself from being hit, put his hands down like lightning and the ball was there.

It was a magnificent catch. So were two by Alan Watkins, one at slip and the other at fine leg, both of which he took diving to leg and holding the ball inches off the ground. Then, of course, we had Jack Ikin, whose close-to-the-wicket fielding is always brilliant, particularly at Old Trafford, Manchester. Jack held three in that match and helped to make that England XI one of the best fielding sides I have seen since the war.

With India dismissed for 58 and 82, we won at Old Trafford by a very convincing margin, and the final Test, at the Oval, was little better—from the visitors' point of view. It must be stated in their favour that rain completely spoiled the game, but they collapsed once more before the bowling of Freddie Trueman and Alec Bedser, and were again dismissed for under 100. Had the weather been brighter, they might have fared better —but I am afraid they were outclassed.

I am quite sure they felt the strain of the bad summer, but this apart, they were disappointing. Frankly, they were not good enough in any sphere of the game. Their batting lacked stability, only the skipper, Hazare, and young Manjrekar putting up any real resistance in the Tests. Their bowling, too, was on the negative side ; steady, but that was all one could say for it, and their fielding was below par.

It was bad luck for them to encounter such " English " weather, but they offered no excuses on that score, and I know from what some of them told me, that they were more than a little disappointed with the show they put up during the summer.

I am sure we shall see a vastly improved side when India next visit us. What a pity it is not until 1959 !

Before passing on to other Tests, I should like to digress just for a few moments.

Lord's holds many very happy memories for me, and none more vivid than those of 1952. As a matter of fact, the name " Lords " has played a very important part in my life, for as I told you in my first book, it was in a house named " Lords " that I lived as a boy. Since the publication of that book, I have been asked many times why it was so called, and whether it had anything to do with cricket.

Let me state quite definitely that the answer is " No ". Lords, at Sheldwich, near Faversham, was not named because of any connection with cricket. My grandfather, a business man with a large family, bought this big old house in the country village. My father was abroad a lot, and my mother not being alive, I lived there with my grandparents, who looked after me from my early boyhood.

As you will see from the photograph of " Lords ", published elsewhere in this book, it was built in three different periods. The centre portion is very early, round about the twelfth century. In fact, so I am told, King John was supposed to have slept in part of the house.

The name " Lords " originated because the Lord of the Manor used to invite notable people there—other Lords, maybe—to dine, and to discuss the business of running the local village. At least, that is the story as I have always known it. The only connection with cricket in that lovely old house was the great enthusiasm for the game shown by its male inhabitants—which included me.

At the end of the war, I married my wife, Jean, and we bought a house in Bearsted, near Maidstone, calling it " The Wickets ". You may know that Bearsted is a very famous Kent village, for some of the earliest cricket recorded in the county was played there.

Its delightful green still provides a lovely setting for the local matches, and its connection with cricket is further strengthened by the well-known players who live in the district. " Tich " Freeman, that wonderful Kent leg-spinner and googly bowler, who still holds so many of the records, lives at " Dunbowlin ", in Bearsted. So does Leslie Ames, that illustrious batsman-wicket-keeper, who really started the era of wicket-keeper-batsmen, for today every stumper is expected to make runs—because of the dual success of Leslie Ames. Well, he lives in a house called " Raylands Mead ", along the Ashford Road, at Bearsted.

After many years at Bearsted, I have now moved to a house called " Wild Acre ", in the Aylesford district, where I hope soon to have a pitch in the garden for the use of my son Howard, who is very keen on the game.

Anyhow, for the people who like looking at other people's houses, you will find photographs (facing p. 48) in this book of " Lords ", " The Wickets ", and " Wild Acre ".

CHAPTER V

1953—The Ashes Regained

A NOTHER VISIT TO THESE SHORES FROM AUSTRALIA—
always an event in the English cricket calendar.
This time, however, the tour assumed an importance
above the normal. That final Test in Australia on our
previous visit " Down Under " had shown that we had
the team to break through their hitherto impregnable
armour, and now the question was—could we keep it
up ? Could we—yes, could we gain those Ashes ?

No wonder the first Test at Nottingham caused almost
unprecedented excitement throughout the whole country,
for it was obvious that the Australians were again a
very fine all-round side, led by Lindsay Hassett, backed
up by those " terrible twins " Ray Lindwall and Keith
Miller.

There was a spirit of grim optimism in the English
camp as we gathered at Trent Bridge for the opening
Test. Australia chose their usual team, except that they
gave a chance to Graham Hole as opening partner to
Arthur Morris. England's selectors chose Don Kenyon
as No. 2 on the batting order, because of his consistent
run-getting for Worcestershire, and as we were still looking for the opening partnership that would emulate the
feats of Len Hutton and Cyril Washbrook, Don looked
the best in the country at that time.

This 1953 series will always be remembered for the fact
that Lindsay Hassett won the toss on all five occasions,
but in the end the " advantage " of the toss proved, as
so often in the past, something of a myth. However,
when Len lost the spin at Nottingham, we anticipated
trouble on that Trent Bridge wicket that had shattered
so many hopes in the past. Yet our doubts were quickly
dispelled. Alec Bedser, bowling with all his old fire (as

he usually does at Trent Bridge), got Graham Hole with the first ball of his second over. Graham uses a rather high back-lift, and Alec bowled him an in-swinging yorker that got through before the bat came down.

A good start indeed, and we hoped for more success, for Arthur Morris, who had been Alec's " rabbit " during the previous tour " Down Under ", started rather shakily. After a few near-misses, however, he weathered his early nerves and settled down to bat very well for 67. Lindsay Hassett, whose rock-like defence we had come to respect, was as steady as ever, and at one stage it looked as though we should never get him out. Yet we were not without our successes, not the least of which was the sending back of Neil Harvey for nought.

Alec Bedser bowled a leg-cutter and Neil played a beautiful leg glide. But he did not get completely over the top of it, a failing with so many left-handed batsmen when they play the leg glide, and Denis Compton, at leg slip, took the ball slap in the tummy. He doubled up, but managed to hang on to it. Good for him, for had Neil stayed, he could have proved a real menace, as he had done so often before.

Anyway, the day finished fairly favourably for England. After a little rain the following morning, the wicket took on new life, and Alec made full use of it. I have never seen anybody who could make the ball " talk " so much as Alec, and on this occasion he was swinging and moving off the pitch to such effect, that he had the Australians in trouble right away.

Trevor Bailey gave him very effective support. I remember having to stand well back to Trevor, for he was bowling really fast just after lunch. Richie Benaud tried a leg glide off a particularly fast ball. Before he connected I anticipated the shot I expected him to play and moved across to the leg side. As Richie deflected the ball, I dived full length to my left and managed to hold the catch on the leg side.

The Australians never recovered, and from 237 for 4 they were all out for 249. It was a startling collapse,

due mainly to Alec Bedser's wonderful bowling. Yet the
sensations were not over by any means, for England
were soon in for some shocks as well.

Don Kenyon tried to hit Lindwall to mid-wicket early
on and was caught. Reg Simpson was l.b.w. for 0,
and Denis Compton was caught by Morris for 0, all three
off Ray Lindwall. We were certainly in trouble right
from the start, and it continued, thanks to bad light and
the bowling of Miller, Lindwall and Hill, who had not
been to England before. A leg-spin bowler with rather
a quick action, Hill did not turn the ball too much but
it seemed to come on to the bat so quickly that there
was always the risk of being l.b.w. One of the chief
characteristics of Hill's bowling, is that he pushes the ball
through quite a lot, and if one does turn, it turns very
quickly and often leaves the batsman stranded.

In that first innings at Trent Bridge we did not achieve
a great deal, although we managed to struggle to 144,
thanks to Johnny Wardle toppling a few over the
boundary. Always a lively character when he is batting,
Johnny hit a couple of sixes and finished up with 29
not out.

When Australia batted again, things soon went our
way. If Arthur Morris had not made 60, they would
really have been in trouble again, but he went for the
bowling and got on top of us. He received scant support, however, and his team mates collapsed once more
against the bowling of Bedser and Roy Tattersall, who
took all the wickets between them. Roy had 3 for 22,
and Alec 7 for 44, to add to his 7 in the first innings.

Incidentally, in that match Alec passed the previous
record of 189 wickets in Test matches, the greatest total
by any other English bowler, and the man whose record
had been surpassed, Sidney Barnes, now aged 80, was
there to see Alec's great achievement, and to offer his
congratulations. It was grand to see these two great
Englishmen together. What history they have written
between them. . . .

There is a story concerning the last stages of the

Australian innings. During that remarkable collapse, the talk in the dressing-room between Lindsay Hassett and his boys was whether they should appeal against the light. They viewed it this way. If their appeal was upheld, Alec would get a much-needed rest, whereas, if they carried on batting, he had been bowling for such a long spell that he might tire quickly.

It was Lindsay Hassett who took the responsibility of solving the problem and he decided to make the appeal rather than risk losing any more valuable wickets. Don Tallon was next man in, and as he was going through the door, Lindsay shouted to him :

" Give it a go, Deafy ! "

Don Tallon, whose nickname is " Deafy " because he is a little hard of hearing, did not realise that Lindsay was referring to the light appeal, and when he started batting, he instantly began to attack the bowling. Eventually he holed out on the boundary.

When he returned to the dressing-room, you can be sure that Lindsay was a little puzzled, not to say annoyed.

" What the hell were you doing, Don ? " the skipper demanded. " You didn't appeal against the light ! "

Don suddenly realised the meaning of these words.

" Crikey ! " he replied. " I thought I was doing as you told me, and giving it a go ! "

The others then realised that Don had misinterpreted his captain's instructions. Instead of appealing against the light, he had " given it a go ", and had lost his wicket.

There is a moral to this story. It is imperative that orders are given concisely by the captain, and not only should the skipper make sure that his orders are understood, but the player himself should also be certain that he understands his instructions.

Australia were all out for 123, which gave us a decided chance. And what a chance, for at close of play that night we were 120 for 1 and only 108 needed to win. . . .

Alas, it was not to be. The following two days were completely rained off, and that was that ! If the game

5

had been played to a finish, I am certain we should
have won. But " ifs " don't win the Ashes. . . . However, we all felt we had made a very good start to the
series and we hoped for better things at Lord's.

Better things did I say? Well, our hopes were
not fulfilled. You will remember what happened.
Although we managed to save a draw, we were really
on the losing end of it, there was no question about that.
Australia were well on top, but thanks to a magnificent
fighting stand in our second innings by Willie Watson
and Trevor Bailey, they were unable to press home
their advantage. We had to bat for the whole of the
last day to save the match, and Willie and Trevor batted
nearly throughout. With half an hour to go, Freddie
Brown and I were left to carry on the battle. Freddie
got 28 runs before he was out in the last over ; a most
valuable innings. It was certainly a dour, grim struggle.
Those Australians made us fight every inch of the
way.

My most notable memory of that Lord's Test was the
umpiring, or rather the decisions that were given in the
match. Umpiring is a very difficult job, and no one
appreciates the difficulties more than I do, but some of
the decisions given in that Test were debatable.

I recall one that puzzled Lindsay Hassett, when I
caught him on the leg side off Brian Statham. From
my point of view, my appeal was not too confident, as
I was not absolutely certain that Lindsay had played
the ball. It is true that it sounded like the ball hitting
the bat, otherwise I would not have appealed at all,
but the appeal was made before I realised that as the
ball had slowed up after passing the bat, and on the
leg side, too, I felt that it might have come off the pad.
Hence the fading of my appeal in a rather half-hearted
way.

There was no doubt in the minds of the slips and
short-leg fielders, however, and I'm afraid my appeal
was drowned in the general chorus. Nor did the umpire
seem in any doubt, for Lindsay was given out.

In the dressing-room at close of play I asked Lindsay if he hit the ball.

" No I didn't," he replied, " and what's more, you know I didn't ! "

On looking back I think he was perhaps right, but at the moment when I caught the ball and made my appeal I was quite confident that he had hit it. It was not until that split second afterwards that I had doubts. However, my colleagues were quite certain that Lindsay had played the ball. It was a difficult decision for the umpire, and, apparently he was wrong. Yet I would not blame him for that—even if I blame the umpires for some of their other decisions.

However, it was not indifferent umpiring that put us in such an awkward position on that last day.

I must pay a tribute to Tom Graveney for his wonderful knock of 78 in our first innings. When we were 177 for 2, thanks to a great stand by Tom and Skipper Len, it really looked as if we had the game in the bag, but as so often has happened, we slipped and then had to fight a backs-to-the-wall battle to save the day.

Never mind, that Test at Lord's was a simply magnificent cricket match—one to be remembered for all time.

Before we pass on to the next Test, I feel I must pay a tribute to Freddie Brown, who was brought back by the selectors, despite some criticism. It was felt in some quarters that it was unfair to choose Freddie, former England captain, to play under Len Hutton. I know Freddie's feelings in the matter, and I think he proved that the selectors were right in their choice.

He pulled his full weight both in bowling, batting and fielding. Mind you, I think there was some doubt as to whether he would be a success, because of the feeling that he has always been susceptible to fast bowling. (Not that I agree !) However, Freddie gave the lie to that one with his 29 invaluable runs against Ray Lindwall. By his audacity and his attacking of the bowling, he saved what looked like certain defeat.

Although we were not in need of runs at that time, there was no reason at all why they should not have been taken when they were there. That is good policy. Hitting fours means that the fielders have to work hard, while nothing gets a bowler's tail down more than to know that the batsman is on top just when the fielding side appears to have the game in control. For that reason alone, Freddie deserved to come back, if only for that one game.

For the third Test at Old Trafford, England made a few changes. Bill Edrich was brought in for Don Kenyon, who had failed, and Reg Simpson was brought back for Freddie Brown, at No. 6. In addition, Brian Statham was suffering from a strained groin, so the opening attack was left to Trevor Bailey and Alec Bedser, with Jim Laker and Johnny Wardle to make use of the Old Trafford pitch when rain affected it, for, of course, Manchester's weather lived up to its reputation !

Lindsay Hassett won the toss and elected to bat on a dampish pitch. Fortunately, there was enough moisture in the wicket for the opening bowlers to get some life out of it, and Alec started in his usual Old Trafford form by bowling both Arthur Morris and Keith Miller with two grand deliveries.

I am not likely to forget this Australian innings. When Neil Harvey came in to bat, he immediately hit Trevor Bailey for 4, and then gave me one of the easiest of catches behind the stumps. I missed it !

It happened like this. I watched the ball off the bat and it looked to me as though it would be a waist-high catch. But the ball must have been travelling a little faster than I expected. Instead of following a normal trajectory, it kept coming up and up, and as it approached, my hands moved farther and farther back into my chest. At last I could not get them any higher, for they were tucked right into my body, and it was too late to step back. So the ball hit the base of my thumbs and bounced out.

Everyone thought I had thrown the ball up before I had really caught it, and it certainly must have looked like that to the onlookers, but it was a miss—no doubt about it.

The catches that look easy from the ring are not always as simple as they may appear to the man trying to hold the ball. How often have I seen a catch go to short-leg and been dropped. The catch has looked simple—to me, but when discussing it with the fielder, the answer usually has been—" the pace of the ball beat me ". In other words, although a fielder is in perfect position to take the catch, the ball travels faster than it appears to the spectator. Believe me, in the middle of a Test, with its tense atmosphere, it is so simple to misjudge a ball, even by a fraction—but it is that fraction that matters. We should not drop catches, I suppose, but a slight misjudgment of pace is just human nature. It happens to all of us.

That particular miss of mine proved most unfortunate for me, and for the team, inasmuch as Neil Harvey went on to make 122. After every scoring stroke I felt I could hear the spectators saying : " If only Evans had caught him when he was four. . . ." I can assure you I was more than thankful when I did catch him eventually, on the leg side, standing up to Alec Bedser. Actually, this was one of the best catches I have made—at least, I thought it was, although that did not make up for that earlier miss. How ironic this game of cricket is !

That was not my only misfortune that day. Alan Davidson, another left-hander, got a fine edge from Jim Laker before he had scored, and once again the ball popped out of my gloves. As before, I gained my revenge by a quick piece of stumping off the same bowler when Alan was 15. It's strange how often the easy chances are missed, yet the difficult ones are taken. Don't ask me why—it just happens.

Thanks in some degree to my misfortunes behind the stumps, Australia finished with 318, a very useful score under the circumstances. It only remained to see what

our batsmen could do on that wicket. We had not long
to wait.

Bill Edrich went very quickly to Hill, caught low
down by Graham Hole, one of the safest catchers in the
game, and almost the equal of Keith Miller. Bill's dismissal brought our two mainstays, Len Hutton and Denis
Compton, together. They put on over 90 together before they both fell late in the day.

Rain made play impossible on the Monday, and when
play resumed on the Tuesday, the wicket was very wet.
However, there was little chance of a decision now, and
our only hope was to get on with the game as quickly as
we could. Well, Reg Simpson hit some beautiful shots,
as only he can when in form, and I had my fair share of
full-blooded cracks to the boundary. In fact, I was
batting when Alec Bedser, last man in, came to the
wicket. We put on 33 together before Arthur Morris
got Alec with one of his " Chinamen ", a rare performance indeed.

You can be sure there was a lot of good-humoured
leg-pulling in the dressing-room afterwards. As you
know, Arthur Morris was Alec's " bunny ", but now it
was Arthur's turn to laugh !

We finished with 276, my own contribution being 44.
Now the wicket was definitely drying out, and this was
to our advantage. When the wicket is too wet, the
ball does not bite into the turf, but now we were looking
forward to seeing Jim Laker and Johnny Wardle doing
their tricks. And they did them . . . !

Jim Laker opened the bowling, and Johnny took over
from Alec after only four overs. Then the fun started.
Wickets dropped like so many skittles. Not one of the
Australians reached double figures, and when the game
ended, they were 35 for 8. What excitement ! It was
really terrific. Remember it ?

The Australians have always been weak in batting on
sticky wickets, and they certainly proved it on that Old
Trafford " patch ". Whether we would have been so
successful had there been another day for play, or whether

we should have won had the game continued for another hour or two that evening, it is impossible to say, but it was certainly exciting while it lasted.

With three Tests gone, and all drawn, we hoped for better things at Leeds. The rain was still hanging around, and when Lindsay Hassett won the toss yet again, he decided to ask us to bat. It was a wise move, as was quickly proved when Ray Lindwall yorked Len Hutton with his second ball. It was a very dull day and when Len returned to the dressing-room, a trifle disconsolate, of course, he admitted that he was unable to pick up the ball against the dim background.

Tom Graveney was in better form, making 55 before Richie Benaud caught him in the gully off Keith Miller. It is unusual to see both Len and Denis Compton with " 0 " against their names in the same innings, but this was one occasion, and I must admit that it did not look too healthy for us when we finished the day with only 142 for 7.

The following morning when Trevor Bailey and I were batting together, I was guilty of running him out. I hit a ball to mid-wicket, and Trevor must have thought there was a quick run in it, for he yelled " Yes ". I did not think there was a chance of a run and said " No ", but Trevor was already well on his way. He and I were well used to one another's running, and when he said " Yes " he took it for granted that I would run. Consequently, when he received my negative call, he turned and made a valiant effort to regain his crease, but the slippery turf was against him, and although he dived full length, bat outflung, he was just a fraction too late. I felt very upset about it, as I always do when there is a run out and I am the cause of it. There are plenty of easy ways of being dismissed when you are batting, without being run out.

Eventually, we scraped up 167, and I felt this was too small a total to give us a fair chance of beating the powerful Australian side, who batted right down to No. 11. However, I had forgotten that Alec Bedser is always at his best when things look blackest, and this was one of those occasions. He bowled magnificently, finishing with 6 for 95—a really great performance.

Tony Lock, having his first bowl in a Test match against Australia, was also in cracking form, although his 1 wicket for 53 runs in 23 overs, was not a true indication of his very fine bowling. Anyway, we kept Australia's lead down to 99, a fair performance, all things being considered.

When we batted again it was unfortunate that rain once more interfered, but Denis and Bill, once nicknamed the " Middlesex twins ", got on top of the Australian attack, and it was mainly due to them that we managed to total 275.

The wicket was now beginning to show signs of turning, and we thought that with any luck we had a good chance of bowling Australia out and forcing a victory. But from the start, with Alec and Tony Lock sharing the attack, it was soon obvious that the tourists were not going to be humiliated in the same way as at Manchester.

Arthur Morris and Neil Harvey attacked the bowling to such good purpose that at one stage it seemed as if they would get the required runs with some ease. With the two left-handers in such forcing form, Len Hutton was faced with a problem. Should he keep his spinners on ? To do so might give us a chance of victory—or it might just as easily provide the Australian batsmen with the means of victory. On the other hand, he could cut down their rate of scoring, and wait for better things in the final Test at the Oval.

Being the cautious type that has made him such a great captain, Len decided on the latter course. It had the desired effect, for Australia were 21 runs short of the winning total when play ended, and they had 6 wickets still to fall. I am well aware that Trevor Bailey bowled his " leg theory " stuff, and it is always difficult to score off this type of bowling, but I still feel that the Australian batsmen should have taken more chances of forcing the runs towards the end of their innings. Of course, it must also be remembered that had they done so, they might have lost their wickets—and lost the Test, so perhaps they, too, were hoping for better things at the Oval.

Four Tests gone—still no result. The Ashes were still in the balance. What a build-up for the last act. It was the sort of situation which most of us only dream about, and the whole country seethed with the excitement.

We were joined by the young fast bowler from York-shire—Freddie Trueman, who had been doing so well during the County season that the selectors had no hesitation in choosing him for this crucial Test. The rest of our attack was made up of Trevor Bailey, Alec Bedser, Tony Lock and Jim Laker. Three bowlers playing on their home ground—it was an advantage which we all hoped would prove a winning card in our own hand.

Australia batted first, yet there was a feeling of real confidence in the whole English team as we took the field. I am quite certain that not one of us had given any thought to defeat, although we knew the strength of the opposition.

Alec Bedser bowled the first ball, and when it pitched on the wicket it made a mark. This was no Oval wicket as we knew it in pre-war days, and I recall Lindsay Has-sett turning to me and saying :

" I don't like the look of that, do you, Godfrey ? "

For my part I was inwardly very pleased. I was certain that our two spinners, Tony and Jim, would be able to make full use of this wicket, whereas their Austra-lian counterparts were not in the same class. It was a pleasing thought.

Freddie Trueman stuck to his task very well, and took four wickets, three of them to me behind the stumps. Helped by Alec and Trevor, we bowled Australia out on that first day for 275, which, although a fair score, was not beyond our range, for we felt we had a strong batting side.

Len gave us a fine start with a well hit 82, and we had 137 on the board for 2 wickets, but then Tom

Graveney and Denis Compton slipped up and we were
170 for 5. Not so good ! So it was up to Trevor and
me to try to repair the damage.

I had not been in very good form with the bat in
County games, and I decided to go in and attack the
bowling, for attack is usually the best form of defence
when one is out of touch. The new ball was taken,
but this did not cause me to alter my decision, and it
succeeded to a certain degree. Trevor and I put on 40,
my share being 28, when our partnership ended all too
suddenly—and, I think, a bit unfortunately.

Ron Archer was bowling, and he had Alan Davidson
at deep fine leg when I was facing the attack, and up to
save the one when Trevor had the strike. A new over
started, and as I was certain I knew the field placings,
I did not trouble to look around. It was foolish of me,
I know, and I regretted it—when it was too late. The
first ball from Ron Archer was just outside the leg stump.
I played it confidently off my legs through the short-
leg field, and immediately set off down the wicket, certain
that it was a safe " two ".

What I didn't know was that Alan Davidson had
forgotten that I was batting, and he was up to save the
one—as he should have been for Trevor Bailey. Trevor
saw me dashing off towards him and immediately yelled :
" No—get back ! "

Instantly I turned, slipped over and slid down the
wicket on my back. Recovering, I dived for the crease.
For a moment I thought I had just made it, but then
I saw Frank Lee's finger go up. Naturally, I was disappointed, for I felt that Trevor and I could have stayed.

Still, we passed Australia's total in the end, Alec
Bedser proving once again that he's not such a bad
batsman with 22 not out. So with 306 on the board,
we had a lead of 31. Not much, you say, but we knew
that even 31 might be useful when we batted last, for
the wicket was now definitely taking spin.

When Australia batted again, Freddie Trueman had
only a couple of overs before Len wisely took him off.

Even Alec Bedser had only a few overs, before the attack was handed over to the Surrey " spin-sters ", Tony Lock and Jim Laker. And how they bowled ! They shared the honours between them, Tony taking 5 for 45, and Jim 4 for 75, and Australia were back in the hutch for the second time with only 162. England needed only 130 runs to win the match and the Ashes urn for the first time for thirty years.

We lost Len at 24, and Peter May at 88, but from then on the game was in the bag. Bill Edrich, always a great fighter, and Denis Compton were there at the end, and it was Denis who made the memorable hit that gave us the series—and the Ashes.

I think it was the finest sight of my life to stand on the balcony at the Oval and see the thousands of delighted spectators, cheering, singing and waving excitedly, as they surged towards the pavilion. And then to stand and look down on that mighty sea of laughing faces as our skipper came out to acknowledge their applause. It was a memory that will live with me through the years.

We had won under the first professional to captain England in a full series against Australia. Len must have felt a very proud man indeed, but not so proud as we felt of him. If ever a man has earned a place on cricket's roll of honour, that man is Len Hutton.

CHAPTER VI

The West Indies Tour—1953–54

WEST INDIES, 1953–54, WAS A SOMEWHAT UNFORTUNATE tour, marred by certain incidents on and off the field that created a disturbance between the players, the Press and the general public. However, we will come to that in its correct sequence.

Our first port of call after leaving England was that beautiful little island of Bermuda, where we played three matches at Hamilton. This, I feel, was a mistake. Bermuda, I should explain, is a long, horse-shoe-shaped island, and very narrow indeed, and as it is only recently that cars have been allowed in Bermuda, most people wishing to cross the island have to do so either by bicycle, by horse or on foot. Only the smallest cars are allowed there at the moment, and these are limited to 15–20 miles per hour all over the island.

So you will see that as we played all three matches at Hamilton, many people on the other side of the island were prevented from seeing the matches. This was a great disappointment to them, and to us. We felt it would have been far better, and would have created a good feeling throughout the country, if we had played one match in each of the three main centres in the island, thus enabling many more people to see the cricket. If this had been done, I am sure the gates would have paid our expenses, and made the Bermuda Cricket Association a profit. As it was, of course, all the matches were played at Hamilton, and because of the travelling difficulties I have enumerated, gates were restricted, and, consequently, the financial result was not all it should have been. Fortunately, Mr. Stanhope Joel, a very wealthy man, came to the rescue and paid our expenses, which amounted to something like £5,000, a very generous gesture indeed.

I enjoyed myself in Bermuda, although the matches did not rank as first-class fixtures. We won the first, and the other two were drawn. Rain and cold weather partially affected the games. My only outstanding memory of the matches is of the first scoring shot I made in the island—a six. Mind you, Hamilton is a small ground and many sixes were hit. It is a matting wicket with a concrete base, making it very lively and very fast, and once the batsman gets going, he can play shots all round the wicket and score very quickly. But if the bowling gets on top, it is difficult to score.

I remember Tony Lock bowling his rather vicious left-arm slows on this matting wicket. He was able to turn the ball quite a bit and was practically unplayable. Against a really good attack on that wicket I do not think any side would score more than 250 runs, and if it was a really fast attack, then it would be difficult to reach even that total, and it would be quite dangerous for the batting side. Still that's how the Bermudans like their cricket.

They are extremely nice people, and very keen on their sport. Naturally, they are very partisan towards their own country, and why shouldn't they be? Aren't we all? Of course there is some kind of colour bar in Bermuda, although it was not too serious, so far as we could see. However, that was none of our business, and we had a very good time. I must admit that I was most impressed with the island. What a lovely place to spend a holiday. I can well understand why it is so popular as a resort for tourists, most of whom come from America.

Bermuda enjoys wonderful weather for most of the year, except for an occasional spell when the temperature drops a little below the sixties, but for nine or ten months of the year, it is in the seventies and eighties, rather like a good English summer. There is wonderful swimming there, perhaps some of the best in the world, and several beautiful golf courses. The Mid-Ocean Golf Course on which we played during our short visit is supposed to be one of the five best in the world. This Bermuda grass is very difficult to putt on owing to the nap, but the lay-out of the course, from a technical point of view, is excellent indeed, and, of course, there is a wonderful Club House.

Yes, the Bermudans look after themselves—and, I must admit, Stanhope Joel looked after us in a right royal manner. He has a beautiful house on Perriot Island, the only house on this tiny island incidentally, which is reached by small motor-boat. He gave us a really wonderful time at his home, and we got to know something of the Bermudans. It was a memorable occasion.

We flew on from Bermuda to Jamaica, where we had a two-day match on a beautiful little ground at Innswood just outside Jamaica. Here we met the great George Headley, the " Black Bradman ", as he used to be known in his hey-day. Leslie Ames has since told me that when he used to keep wicket behind him, he thought he was one of the greatest batsmen ever. The public in Jamaica think so much of George Headley that they subscribed over £1,000 to bring him back to Jamaica from England especially to play against us, which shows you how patriotic the Jamaicans are about their own particular players. Unfortunately, he was hit on the elbow in this game, which kept him out of the first Jamaican colony match, so his supporters did not really have an opportunity of seeing George Headley at his best.

When we started this tour, England were virtually leaders in the world of cricket because we had just beaten Australia. On the other hand, the West Indies had been beaten by Australia by only a close margin, after the West Indians had beaten England in their last visit here. So the forthcoming Test series really devolved into a battle for world supremacy, because if the West Indies beat us, they would assume the virtual position of leadership in world cricketing circles.

One must admit, however, that there was more to it than this. With the West Indians being predominantly coloured, a certain racial prejudice entered into the question, and the Tests became virtually a contest between " white " and " coloured ". I hope I hurt no one's feelings in making such a statement—I do not intend to—but there is no question about it at all that a certain section of the people, and the Press out there, did their best to build up the political aspect of the Tests and caused a certain amount of feeling between the two sides to suggest that we were playing something more than a contest between bat and ball.

The troublous undercurrent was obvious even in our opening first-class match in Jamaica, at Sabina Park. Every time a home player scored runs, or later, whenever one of our wickets fell, thunder-flashes would burst out all over the ground, creating a terrific uproar. At times it seemed as if we were playing cricket on the Dunkirk beach head ! It was cricket played under tension, and we all felt it. Obviously, we had to do our best to win, but this subtle form of opposition made it very difficult at times for us to maintain the calm dignity and cricket tradition expected of an M.C.C. touring side.

Sabina Park is a beautiful ground in Kingston, and with the flags fluttering in the gentle breeze above the pavilion, and the crowds all in shirts of varied rainbow colours, it presented a delightful scene. If only the cricket atmosphere could have been as delightful. . . .

In this first Colony match Len Hutton won the toss, and it was quite debatable whether we should bat or put the Jamaicans in. Well, Len decided to ask Jamaica to bat. This, I think, is the right policy when a team is newly arrived in a country, as the boys are not quite acclimatised to the light, and not fully accustomed to the wickets. It takes time to get used to the pace at which the ball comes through and how it will react in different circumstances. Thus, if a skipper wins the toss and puts the opposition in, it gives his men an opportunity of a spell in the field, to get the feel of the turf, and accustom themselves to the light. Even when the home side score runs fairly freely—as they did on this occasion—I still think Len's policy was right.

In actual fact, the Jamaicans were 220 for 4 at one stage, but we finished them off for 266. We had a fastish attack with Trueman, Statham, and Trevor

Bailey, who between them did most of the bowling. Tony Lock bowled a bit and was quite successful, getting 2 for 59 in 28 overs, but Jim Laker was kept in reserve, for obviously the wicket did not suit him, being hard, fast and true. We thought we did very well to get Jamaica out for such a small score, but when it was our turn to bat, there was a doubt as to who should open. Well, Willie Watson was given the job with Len, and the Yorkshireman was in cracking form. He was obviously the opening batsman we were looking for, and of our grand score of 457 for 7 declared, Willie scored a beautiful 161. On the whole we had a jolly good day's batting, everybody getting a little practice except Peter May, who was bowled for 9, and myself—stumped for nought !

Jamaica batted again, and this time our fast attack really got going. Freddy Trueman was now working up a bit of pace and was showing really good form, and Statham—well, Statham is always reliable, and Jamaica were bowled out for 170, giving us an innings victory, a good start.

We felt that winning the first major match of the tour, gave us a slight psychological advantage over the opposition, although, of course, this was not a Test side. However, this was the first time Jamaica has been beaten at Sabina Park for many a long day, the first time, I think, since Yorkshire did it, way back in 1936.

The second match in Jamaica went very much the same way as the first, except that George Headley was playing, and, of course, the crowds absolutely flocked to see their idol. Once again Jamaica made a good start and they were 103 for 2, Frederick doing most of the damage. He did not look all that good a batsman, but for some unaccountable reason he got quite a stack of runs in those early matches against us, and it seemed as though he might earn a Test place.

I shall never forget the moment when George Headley came in. The crowd went frantic, jumping up in their seats, cheering, hooting and creating the most tremendous din. When George got off the mark, with a single to cover, another even more deafening roar went up. Then he suddenly hit one for four, a jolly good shot it was, too, and this time the crowd literally went wild. Freddy Trueman next bowled him one short pitched, a bouncer. George got behind it and hooked it like a rocket. Ken Suttle, fielding at fine leg, chased after it and caught the ball brilliantly in the outfield. George Headley was out, and the result was sensational. You could have heard a pin drop. There was not the slightest sound anywhere in the ground, and I'm afraid Ken Suttle's brilliant catch was not appreciated.

George Headley's dismissal was a disheartening blow and it seemed to get the team right down. Alan Moss, our fast bowler, giving Statham a rest, and Trueman bowled really well. They got on top of the batting and eventually Jamaica were all out for 187. Moss took 4 for 47 in 18 overs, a really good start to his first tour.

When we batted, Peter May got going and hit a brilliant 124. He did not give a chance and we finished 99 on with 286. Jamaica were not finished, however, and in that second innings they fought back very well. This time it was Holt and George Headley who saved the day.

You can guess that pleased the crowd no end ! George stayed for about three hours for his 53, an innings that not only helped to save Jamaica from defeat, but eventually gained him his Test place.

I remember Holt's innings. When he was 33 I caught him off a hard snick from Johnny Wardle—but the umpire gave him not out ! Oh dear, was I sorry ! He went on to make 152 and saved the match. . . . Still, that is one of those things that happen. Umpires are only human. In any case, in this particular instance the umpire said that the bowler walked across his wicket and obscured the umpire's vision as the batsman played the ball. Well, if that was so, the umpire had no option but to give Holt not out, because he did not see what happened. It was bad luck for Johnny because that wicket might have given us a chance of victory.

6

With the finish of that match, the tension began to mount. The first Test was due, and the whole of the West Indies were in a ferment of excitement. People came from all the islands, and long before the game was due there was no accommodation left in the town. Kingston is quite a large place, with very palatial hotels, but every spare corner was booked up for the match.

The whole match was fought out under tension, but owing to the Press and the loud-speakers on the ground appealing to the crowds to curb their enthusiasm so far as thunder-flashes were concerned, we had no interruptions of that nature. But that does not mean to say there was no excitement. You cannot keep a West Indies cricket crowd quiet, especially when a Test match is being played.

The atmosphere was a little strained. I remember a spot of trouble in relation to Test tickets for our English friends in the West Indies. It was during this Test in Jamaica that Sam Peskin and his two sons came over from their hotel, Gloucester House in Montego Bay, but were unable to obtain tickets. As Sam had so kindly invited Len and Mrs. Hutton, Denis and Mrs. Compton and my wife and I, to be his guests while our ladies were on that side of the island, we naturally wished to give him the best possible seats. But as our tickets had already been given away owing to the short notice of his arrival on the Test scene, we asked him if he would come and sit in the places reserved for players in the pavilion.

On entering the pavilion we met the secretary, Mr. Rae, who would not hear of our request. There was something of a scene, but eventually, however, the trouble was overcome and we were able to take Sam and his family in, and gave them a good day. Which shows that Test tickets are very difficult to obtain by the players even for their own personal friends.

It was a beautiful wicket. George Headley was in the side, but the famous West Indian " W " trio was broken. Everton Weekes and Clyde Walcott were both in, but Frankie Worrell was not very well and could not play, so Frederick took his place. They also had a wicket-keeper, McWatt, whom we had not seen before. Sonny Ramadhin was in, too, and Valentine, those two great bowlers who did so much damage in England on their last visit. So they had a pretty good side with Jeff Stollmeyer, the skipper, and Gerry Gomez.

West Indies batted first, and got away to a good start. Jeff Stollmeyer made a beautiful 60. He's a most graceful player, and a grand cricketer, but for some unaccountable reason he was not popular in Jamaica as skipper. Why, I do not know, unless it was that they preferred a Jamaican to be captain in Jamaica, although I cannot see that point really. Jeff's tactics came in for a lot of criticism from the public and the Press, which appeared to me to be most unfair.

Holt was unfortunate enough to miss his hundred. He was 94 when Statham bowled him a very slow bouncer. It was a perfectly straight ball but it was very short and it would have hit about a foot up from the base of the stumps. Holt got into position to hook it, but he was far too early. The ball hit him on the pad, and, of course, he was out. There was no question about it and the umpire had no hesitation whatever in giving him out.

I am afraid that decision, fair as it was, received a bad reception—and so did the umpire. It was reported that his wife was attacked on the ground, his father assaulted at work, and his young lad thrown into the river going to school the following morning, and all because he gave Holt out at 94 instead of letting him go on to his hundred. Is it any wonder that there are bad decisions given in the West Indies? I was not surprised, when I caught Holt twice in the British Guiana Test, and he was given " not out " on each occasion. Umpiring is difficult enough without the crowds making the job harder.

Eventually, West Indies were all out for 417. This was not excessive under the circumstances, for, after all, the wicket was still playing very well and we had a good chance to make an effective reply. Unfortunately we did not ! Ramadhin and Valentine came in for their usual share of wickets, ably assisted by Gerry Gomez, with his medium-pace in-swingers and away-swingers. He bowls rather like Charlie Palmer these days. He is very medium pace, with a not very long run-up, and makes the ball swing and move in the air. He bowled really well in that innings and took 3 for 16 in 9 overs, which was extremely good on that very hard wicket.

We were all out for 170, and now the question was whether Jeff Stollmeyer would make us follow-on. With such a lead, they could easily have made us bat again, but Jeff elected to bat himself instead of making us follow-on. That decision was greeted with extreme disapproval by the crowd, and every time he came on to the field after that, there was loud and persistent booing. There was even a gun-fight over in the corner of the ground reserved for coloured spectators!

In the West Indies they bet on everything, and I suppose many people had bet that their favourites would win by an innings, so when Jeff Stollmeyer decided to bat again, this may have had much to do with the disturbance. That decision also created considerable ill-feeling among the players, because some of them felt that Jeff should have made us follow-on. In consequence, poor Jeff came in for tremendous hostility from his own crowd—from everybody really, except us!

So far as we were concerned, we realised that the onus was now on the West Indies, and in that second innings we did quite well. But for Everton Weekes making a brilliant 90, we should have had them in trouble. Jeff Stollmeyer eventually declared at 209 for 6, leaving a day and a half for them to bowl us out, or for us to get the runs. Mind you, it was a tall order to make 457 to win, but it had been done before and there was no reason why it should not be done again, for the wicket was still in excellent shape.

We made a magnificent start, thanks to Willie Watson and Len Hutton, and we had 130 on the board for 1. Len was l.b.w. to Gomez, one of those little swingers that came in off the pitch and just beat the bat. Peter May followed and began playing brilliantly. At this time the crowd were very quiet. They always are when things are going against their side. As our score rose to 220 for 1 the silence grew more and more tense. Then came another wicket, McWatt caught Peter May off Frank Kentish. That success was greeted with tremendous cheers, and the spirits of the crowd rose incredibly.

The players had been a little dispirited too, but with the encouragement from their supporters they began to bowl very well again. Ramadhin came back and immediately bowled Denis Compton. This was a misfortune, but we were still in a good position with 282 for 4. Victory was not a lost cause by any means—or rather it should not have been—but then we completely collapsed and lost the match.

Whether I was the cause—or part of the cause—for our defeat, I leave you to decide, but here is the story of what happened. We naturally were invited by the local people to attend various social functions, and on the evening before the last day of the Test I was invited by Colonel and Mrs. Simpson to a party at Blue Mountain Inn. This is a wonderful little inn up in the hills just outside Jamaica. I was looking forward to it very much, for I thought it would be a chance to relax for a short time before the last day of the Test match. During the afternoon, skipper Len Hutton came to me and said :

" Look, Godfrey, I don't want you to go to that party tonight. I want you to get to bed early in view of the fact that you will be batting tomorrow."

Now I felt this instruction to be unnecessary, for I was an experienced tourist, and should not need to be told when to go to bed. I was very upset, but I said :

" All right, if that is your wish, I'll do as you say."

After all, Len was our 'captain, and the last thing I would wish to do would be to disobey what was virtually an order. So off to bed I went at ten o'clock, but the incident had so upset me that I couldn't sleep for hours.

Eventually, however, I did drop off, but next morning

I felt a bit jaded. Maybe I should have forgotten the whole incident, except that I heard someone say that Len Hutton had been to the party in my place.

Well, of course, this made me really angry, so angry, in fact, that I let it get the better of me. Not that I made any complaint to Len, but I allowed the incident to upset my whole attitude to my cricket, and ruin my mental reaction and concentration. When I went in to bat I had no heart for the job, and I was bowled by Kentish for nought. I had failed hopelessly when I might have done enough to give us a chance of winning the match. Blame me if you will, but I relate the incident to show how one small thing can completely upset a batsman's concentration—and also affect the result of a match—just because I thought my captain had let me down. In the end I am glad to say the whole matter was straightened out quite amicably.

When I tackled Len about it, he said :

" Well, I thought that as you were batting, it would be better for you to have a nice rest in bed than to go out. I'm sorry if I upset you ! "

Not a bit—it was for me to be sorry, and I apologised. Never before had I resented an order from my captain, and I realised how wrong I was. Where would be the spirit of a team if all the players refused to heed the instructions of the skipper ?

This is even more important when, as in this particular case, Len was captaining a Test side overseas for the first time. This brings to light the point that a captain in England meets his players the day before the Test and during the match and virtually has no contact with their social or outside life, whereas on tour, the captain lives with his players both on and off the field, and incidents such as mine can only be tackled through experience. Maybe this incident gave Len food for thought and perhaps made him realise that each player must be handled as a separate individual, a task that he mastered so well later on, that the side recovered from early setbacks to draw level in the series, and such faith had we in the maestro that he even succeeded in retaining the Ashes in Australia.

It was unfortunate that we lost the Test, but fortunately the whole rather regrettable incident was forgotten. From then on, of course, Len and I were great pals, as we had always been, and, as you know, our wives joined us in Jamaica at the end of the tour, and we had a grand time together. It just goes to show that a player must not let any personal matter interfere with his cricket—for such incidents only upset the whole side in some degree.

Having lost the first Test, there were three more to go, so we still had a chance.

From Kingston we visited Antigua, an entirely new spot for me, in the Leeward Islands. It is a beautiful little island, and although there is not much to do, the weather is usually magnificent. We were only there for four days, but we thoroughly enjoyed the trip. The boys had a wonderful time on the cricket field. Johnny Wardle gave the crowd a real thrill with his antics in catching the ball, throwing it, hitting it here, there and everywhere, juggling it with his feet, and getting up to all sorts of tricks. The crowd absolutely loved it, and I'm certain they learnt a tremendous lot about cricket.

We played a two-day match on the island, and there was a full house on both days, which meant that the local cricket clubs made some money, which was pleasing to us, for, after all, we were really out there to encourage their cricket. As Freddy Trueman and I were not playing we made a trip right across the island to a wonderful place called Deep Water Bay. It was about two miles wide, as calm as a sheet of glass, but apparently very deep indeed. There was a lovely sandy shore about thirty yards in depth, and although it dropped sheer into very deep water, it was perfect for swimming.

To get there, we drove right across the island, and it was just like going on a Monte Carlo Rally, for there was no real road, only little tracks, some very rough. But we had a great day, and I can assure you that Fred and I were extremely tired when we got back.

However, it was really a wonderfully refreshing respite
from the strain of cricket and the tension of the Test
match, and did us both no end of good.

Next we flew down to Barbados, probably the strongest
of the West Indies teams. As soon as we arrived, everybody wanted to see the famous Yacht Club with its sandy
beach, and it was not long before we were having a game
of football on the sands. But this did not last long.
Johnny Wardle twisted his knee in trying to score a
hypothetical goal, and I stubbed my toe in the sand and
nearly broke it, so we called it a day. Football on the
sands is not quite the thing to do when you're on a Test
tour.

Incidentally, later in the tour, we went to the Wind-
ward Islands, where, at Grenada, we had a two-day
fixture on a fast matting wicket. The standard of play
here was much higher than that at Antigua, and the team
included a fast bowler who, given more opportunity in
higher class cricket would, I am sure, have made the Test
side. His name at the moment eludes me, but this strap-
ping six-foot six-inch young man had a rhythmic action
and follow-through as good as any we saw on the tour.

Here we had an opportunity to visit the natural har-
bour, where Lord Nelson hid his Fleet when the dangers
to the Royal Navy were apparent in those days. This
was one of the most interesting days from an historical
point of view on the whole of the tour. The Navy took
us for a trip round the bay, where the boys had a swim,
diving from the ship's side, a most exhilarating experience
as they had no costumes !

In Jamaica I had a cyst on my shoulder and the doctors
advised me to have it out. So after the Test I went along
to the local hospital and under a local anaesthetic the job
was done. The doctors were cutting and sawing away
for an hour or more. It was not a pleasant experience
and I certainly did not feel very well after it—nor before
it, come to that. This might have had some bearing on
the fact that my temperament was a little on edge and I
took offence at things that normally would not have upset

me at all. On reflection I feel this definitely had something to do with that little misunderstanding I had with Len Hutton. So perhaps it was *my* fault and not his.

Barbados is a wonderful island. We played one match there, against Barbados, prior to the second Test. Barbados had not been beaten for fifty-odd years and eventually we won by one wicket. It was a terrifically exciting match. Unfortunately, because of the cyst, I was unable to play, so my co-partner, Dick Spooner, kept wicket.

On the whole, the boys put up a good show. Barbados, batting first, scored 389 with the help of Denis Atkinson, who made a brilliant 151. Denis is an all-rounder rather like Keith Miller, and a great cricketer, too. He is very enthusiastic in the field ; has a similar bowling action to Keith, although not as fast, more like medium pace, and he sometimes bowls the off-spinner type of ball ; and is a hard-hitting right-handed batsman when he gets going. He certainly got going here. We followed with 373, just a few short of their total, so we were still in the running. In the second innings Lock and Laker came into their own and Barbados were bowled out for only 179, leaving us 196 to win. We got them with Freddy Trueman and Alan Moss in a last-wicket stand, and it was a leg bye, I think, that eventually won the match. Yes, it was certainly exciting.

Having beaten Barbados, we reckoned we had a good chance of winning the second Test at Bridgetown, and I think we would have done, if it had not been for Clyde Walcott's terrific innings of 220. It was during this match that I watched the best cricket I have ever seen in my life. In one particular over, bowled by Trevor Bailey, every ball was a good delivery, but Clyde Walcott was batting like a master. He hit every ball like a rocket, yet every one of those fierce drives was fielded. There was no run scored off that over, yet it was brilliant cricket. Six different strokes were beautifully played by Clyde Walcott, right in the middle of the bat. Six different balls were bowled by Trevor, each a good 'un, and each ball brilliantly fielded in different parts of the field. That is why I say that it was the greatest over I had ever seen, even though it was a maiden. So, remember, runs don't always make for great cricket.

Clyde certainly DID score runs, however, and he and Bruce Pairaudeau put up a magnificent stand. Pairaudeau's collection was 71 and all-rounder Denis Atkinson helped out with 53. So to get the West Indies out for 383 was a pretty good performance, considering Clyde Walcott had scored 220 of them off his own bat.

When we batted, things happened, and we fell into a rut. The batting was not really all that bad, but we did not score runs. Ramadhin and Valentine were allowed to bowl over after over, maiden after maiden, in fact out of the 104 overs they bowled, 60 were maidens. Tom Graveney, usually a great stroke maker, fell to a full toss because he seemed frightened to hit the ball for four. He should have played his natural game. Len Hutton, at the other end, is always a little slow because that's the way he has been taught to bat, but that was no reason why the rest of the team should try to follow his example. They were just trying to stay there instead of scoring runs, and, in consequence, we only made 181.

It was not very good, especially in view of the fact that the West Indies batted even better in their second innings. Holt made 166, but unfortunately Jeff Stollmeyer was run out—his second run-out in the match. He and Holt were opening for the first time in that match and were not yet accustomed to one another's ways at the wicket. Frank Worrell did well, too, after being bowled by Statham for nought in the first innings, and this time got a not out 76. Eventually they declared at 292 for 2, leaving us with a real struggle on our hands.

Willie Watson was soon " caught McWatt bowled King " for nought. That was a bad start. But Len Hutton, whose 72 in the first innings occupied 4½ hours, got 77 in the second and he and Peter May put on over 100 between them, while Denis came in with 93. His wife, Valerie, had just joined him and he was in tip-top form. Tom Graveney also batted much better in the second innings, and he was 64 not out. Our hopes brightened at one time for we were 258 for 4 at one stage, but I'm afraid we faded away again. As our last batsman, I could not get going at all and Sonny Ramadhin bowled me with one that kept a bit low. Eventually we were out for 313, losing the match by 181 runs.

That meant we were two down with three to play. We knew we were in for a struggle, for the West Indians were right on top now, and once they get on top they take a bit of shifting.

From the beautiful island of Barbados we moved to the difficult mainland of British Guiana—and it was here that we really started getting on top of the bowling. We realised that the policy of slow, careful batting was getting us nowhere, so we decided to get on with it and try to change our fortunes. In consequence, in the Colony match at Georgetown, Willie Watson scored 257 and Tom Graveney 231, and we eventually got 607. We bowled British Guiana out twice and won the match by an innings. That put our tails up again and gave us new confidence for the third Test, which was vital to us, for we had got to win to uphold our prestige.

Fortune followed the brave. We won the toss and Len Hutton scored a magnificent 169, helped by Denis who got 64, and Johnny Wardle with 38. Trevor Bailey hit 49 and I stayed a little while for 19. We totalled 435, a more than useful score.

Now came the West Indies, and Frankie Worrell opened. Now Frank wasn't the master batsman we knew in 1950. He was a bit susceptible to Statham, whose power and pace was increasing with every match, and Frank gave me a catch in the first over. It was a grand start. Then Brian bowled Skipper Stollmeyer and Clyde Walcott with an absolute beauty that came back and got the inside edge of the bat as Clyde tried to hit it through the covers. This was better than we had hoped for—3 for 16. Everton Weekes played a great innings and hit 94 before Tony Lock bowled him, but eventually we got them out for 251, and made them follow-on.

We had their tails down and Frankie gave me another
catch off Statham. Another great start for us. Holt
followed his 48 not out in the first innings with 64 in the
second. I remember catching him off Trevor Bailey in
the first, and I caught him again off Statham in the
second, but both appeals were turned down ! Were we
angry at the time ? This, of course, was the Test match,
too, where the bottles started flying, when McWatt was
run out by Peter May in the first innings, when he
was 54.

He and Holt had put on 98 runs, and thus wanted
only two to put up a hundred partnership. I suppose all
the enthusiastic coloured boys in the crowd bet on this.
Then McWatt cut one down to a close third man where
Peter May was fielding. They took a single and then
with the crowd yelling " Two, two, two—for the hundred ! " they turned for a second. Peter May picked the
ball up beautifully, flung it to me like a rocket and while
the two batsmen were scampering down the wicket, I
caught the ball and whipped off the bails. McWatt was
at least three yards out of his ground. There was no
doubt about the decision. The umpire raised his finger,
and back went McWatt to the pavilion.

That started the rioting. They wanted to know why
McWatt was given out. On a previous occasion Robert
Christiani had been caught at mid-wicket by Willie
Watson off Jim Laker, Willie dived forward and took the
ball a few feet off the ground, and the crowd thought that
because the umpire was a little slow in giving his decision
that Christiani should not have been given out. Then
had come the McWatt run-out. They showed they did
not like it at all, and the umpire came in for a storm of
criticism. Then the bottles started flying and play was
held up for quite a long time while the bottles were
cleared.

The scenes were really alarming, so much so that the
President of the Board of Control in British Guiana asked
Len Hutton if he would like to take his men off the field.
Len quite rightly said :

" No, we want to win this match. It's our one chance to win the series."

So we stayed, the din died down and eventually we got another wicket, which finished off the West Indies for 251. As I have said, we made them follow-on and bowled them out again for 256. So with only 73 wanted to win, we did it with the loss of just one wicket. Peter May was bowled by Atkinson for 12, but Willie Watson and Tom Graveney knocked off the runs and that made two to one in the series with two to play.

I shall never forget that Test match in British Guiana as long as I live. It certainly created a sensation in the West Indies, and it was certainly a bad show while it lasted, but I think perhaps in the long run it has done cricket in the West Indies a tremendous lot of good. At the time they thought they were good sports when all of a sudden came this rioting and throwing of bottles at the English players. Both Press and radio condemned this behaviour with such good effect, that from then on the Test was played in much happier circumstances, and there was no further trouble of any serious nature.

From Georgetown we went on to Trinidad. It was here that I unfortunately picked up a germ in my foot. I developed a tremendous boil or carbuncle, and spent a week in the hotel room having penicillin treatment. I missed the game against Trinidad and the fourth Test match at Port o' Spain, and went from there direct to Jamaica for the final Test. We drew the Test in Trinidad, a tremendous scoring game. Over 1,500 runs were scored on the jute matting. Incidentally this was the last Test to be played there on matting, for the pitch is now a grass one.

With a draw in Trinidad, we went to the fifth and final Test in Jamaica needing to win to share the series. Well, you know the story. We won quite easily. The West Indies won the toss and elected to bat on a lovely wicket, but Trevor Bailey came into his own and put up a really wonderful performance, taking 7 for 34 in 16 overs. We got them out for 139 and then we replied with 414. Len

Hutton contributed 205, Johnny Wardle 66, and I stayed
in for about three hours and managed to get 28. We
bowled the West Indies out again for 346 and finished
with 72 for 1 to give us a win to draw the series.

After a disappointing start, we blended into a winning
team. Certainly at the finish it was the West Indians
who were panicking over their selections and it gave the
Europeans in the islands a tremendous fillip when we
fought back to draw what was one of the hardest series
of matches ever played in international cricket, and for
this recovery we must accord a vote of thanks to our
captain Len Hutton. He was a great skipper and a
worthy ambassador under the most difficult and em-
barrassing conditions.

CHAPTER VII

Pakistan, 1954—"Fazal's Test"

AFTER THE STRENUOUS TOUR OF THE WEST INDIES, WE returned to England expecting 1954 to be a fairly easy summer, for Pakistan were due to make their first appearance in England as a side of Test status. I mean no disrespect to the Pakistanis when I say that we looked forward to a fairly easy summer, but we knew they were not very strong, for they themselves admitted their limitations.

After my rather up and down tour of the West Indies, I felt very much fitter by the time the new season started, and personally I looked forward to the 1954 English summer to complete my recuperation. Actually, I felt right on top form from the start, and in our opening Championship game, at Gravesend, against Derbyshire, I scored 109 in the first innings. It was a most encouraging start to the season for me, and gave me thoughts of a really successful summer.

I remember one particular incident in that innings. Cliff Gladwin, an old Test colleague of mine, was bowling with a new ball. He's an in-swing bowler and a good one, too, but for some unaccountable reason, I connected with a number of leg-side shots and scored 15 off the first over. Cliff glared at me and growled in mock anger :

" What are you doing, Evans ? What do you think you're about ? "

" Sorry, Cliff," I replied, " I'm just having a bit of luck ! "

The next over he bowled me was a maiden, and as he passed me at the change-over he said :

" Your luck didn't last long ! "

But I found my form again in the following over and clumped him for 15, so Donald Carr, the Derbyshire captain, called across to him :

" You'd better put your sweater on, Cliff."

" Thanks ! " said Cliff, " I've had enough of this chap Evans ! "

He had his revenge, however, in the second innings, when he had me caught by Derek Morgan in the leg trap from one of his in-swingers, which I had been hitting for fours in the first innings. Still, that's the fun of the game.

In the following match, also at Gravesend, we had a very exciting finish, for Worcestershire declared leaving us 331 to get in about 250 minutes. We were up against Reg Perks and a first-rate Worcester attack, and the wicket was still good. Personally, I did not think we had any chance of getting the runs, but Skipper Doug Wright's orders were to have a go. After a slowish start, we gradually began to push the score on in an effort to catch up on the clock. Mind you, Gravesend is a very fast ground as everyone knows. It is fairly small, and there is a slope to one side, so that once the ball has passed the fielder, it travels quite fast to the boundary.

With four wickets down, I joined one of our Colts, Ted Witherden, and we were soon scoring at well over a run a minute.

I particularly enjoyed this innings, because Reg Perks was bowling for much of the time I was at the wicket. Reg has always been a great character, and whenever we met we usually had a quiet bet together about hitting sixes, because, as you all know, left-hander Reg always believed in hitting the ball as hard and as far as he could —that is if he hit it at all ! Anyway, in this match at Gravesend, the usual bet was on, but in the second innings, Reg " holed out " just in front of the sight-screen. So I had nothing to pay out !

Then it was my turn and as I took my place at the wicket, I looked enquiringly at Reg and with a wink he said :

" Usual, Godfrey ! "

During one over from Reg, I happened to see one come down just right. It was well pitched up and I had an almighty crack at it. The ball soared straight over the sight screen for six. As Reg stood clapping the shot, I called to him :

" That's a shilling you owe me ! "

At last we wanted about eight runs to win in the last over, or very nearly the last.   Reg was still bowling when he tossed me down a similar type of ball to the other. I hit it right in the meat and it cleared the ground for another six to win the match.

Perks, a grand sport, came into the dressing-room to offer his congratulations, and then turned to me :

" I congratulate you, too, Godfrey, even though you have collected a couple of bob from me for those two sixes ! "

But my apologies for those diversions, so now let's get on to the Pakistan tour.   Well, you may remember that 1954 was one of the worst summers in England for many years.   The weather was very bad and, in consequence, it was hardly a fair test for the Pakistanis, especially as this was their first touring season in international cricket. I can imagine how they must have felt when the first three days of the opening Test at Lord's were completely rained off.   This surprised us too, for such a long delay had seldom happened before at cricket's headquarters. The rain had its compensations, however, for it brought me one of the most memorable incidents of my whole career.

The Queen and the Duke of Edinburgh were due to visit Lord's on the Saturday to meet the players, but owing to the continuous rain, this was impossible.   Our disappointment was changed to delight, however, when we heard that Her Majesty had invited both teams to Buckingham Palace.   How wonderful !   The Queen and the Duke met us most informally in their own lovely home, and stood chatting for nearly an hour.   I think it was a truly gracious gesture of Her Majesty to invite us to the Palace, and I know that none of us present on that historic occasion will ever forget it.   I am sure I shall not, for it was the first time I had ever been inside the Palace. This would have been memorable enough, but it was the homely, informal atmosphere of that visit that made it such a wonderful experience, and one of the highlights of my career.

7

The rain ceased over the week-end and we made a start to the first Test on the Monday after lunch. Len won the toss and decided that the only chance we had of winning the match was to put the Pakistanis in to bat and get them out quickly. However, it was only a slender chance and few of us really felt that the match would be completed in the curtailed time available.

On that very soft wicket, Pakistan began reasonably well. Hanif Mohammad, a little fellow with a very sound defence, and Alim-Ud-Din started off very steadily, as though determined to get as much practice as possible on the wet wicket against our bowlers. They had never faced anyone quite so fast and so accurate as Brian Statham, and they obviously wanted to get used to him before taking any risks. The pitch did not help us much until, all of a sudden Alim-Ud-Din was caught by Bill Edrich off a Johnny Wardle spinner that turned a bit. That was the start. The Pakistanis were in trouble, and from then on we never looked back. On the Monday, Brian had a magnificent spell, capturing the last four wickets for the very small sum of 10 runs—3 in 13 balls ! It was bad luck on the tourists for the wicket was very different from what they were used to in their own country, and eventually we had them out for 87.

With still a chance of victory, our instructions from Len were to get on with it as quickly as possible and go all out to attack the bowling. It was not all that easy, however, because although this was Pakistan's first international tour of England, the team had some very useful bowlers. Some had played in the Lancashire League and were well acclimatised to the grounds in the north, which are often on the damp side, similar to this one at Lord's. In consequence, they used the ball to considerable advantage. Actually, Khan Mohammad and Fazal Mahmood bowled unchanged—Khan was their fastest bowler, a little quicker than Trevor Bailey but not so fast as Statham or Tyson. Fazal, the Alec Bedser type, who bowls swingers and cutters, is one of the best of his type in the world today.

Well, he and Khan gave us a few shocks. Len Hutton and Denis Compton were both bowled for nought, but Reg Simpson and Peter May managed to stay for a time. Reg played a characteristic innings, full of beautiful shots, but it was all too short. However he made 40 very useful runs. Peter got 27 and I managed to collect 25. Eventually Len declared at 117 for 9, obviously with the intention of trying to put the tourists out for a second time and then getting the few runs necessary for victory.

The intention was right, but the result was a little disappointing. Although Alim-Ud-Din was bowled by Trevor Bailey with no runs on the board, little Hanif and Waqar Hassan put on 71, and with Maqsood Ahmed collecting 29, our chance of a quick victory was shattered. Hanif was out off the last ball of the match. He certainly made a great impression on all of us, for during the match he was at the wicket for 340 minutes for 59 runs, a really remarkable performance from so young a batsman on such a bad wicket.

To return for a moment to Alim-Ud-Din's dismissal, when Trevor sent his off-stump cartwheeling out of the ground. I always think it is a wonderful sight to see a stump flying out of the ground from a fast bowler. It gives a great thrill to the spectators I'm sure, and I should like to see more of it. I suggest that it would be a good idea, when the wicket is really hard, for the stump sockets to be watered. If this was done, it would not affect the wicket in any way, but when a really fast ball hit the wicket, a stump would be whipped out of the ground. Thrills for all ! Why not ?

The result of that first Test at Lord's, although disappointing, was heartening to the tourists, and, in consequence, they looked forward to the second Test at Nottingham. If only the weather would brighten up—

Changes were made in the England team, Appleyard and Graveney coming in for Tattersall and Edrich, and, of course, Len Hutton not being well, David Sheppard took over as captain. On paper, this looked a fairly powerful side. Pakistan included Khalid Hassan, who, at 16, was the youngest player ever to appear in a Test match.   A little leg-spinner, he was unfortunate to make his bowling debut when Denis Compton was at his best on a pretty good wicket.

Before this happened, however, Pakistan won the toss and as the weather was fine—for a change—it seemed that they had a good chance of making a good score.   But I'm afraid they missed their chance.   After a steady start, the batsmen failed.   Statham managed to get a wicket early on, and then Bob Appleyard was given his first over in Test cricket.   It was a sensational debut.   With his second ball he had Hanif l.b.w.   It was just the inspiration he needed and he never looked back.   He bowled Waqar Hassan ;   I managed to catch Maqsood off him, and then he bowled Imtiaz Ahmed, all in the space of about three overs.

Why was it that these Pakistanis crumpled against the bowling of Appleyard ?   From my position behind the stumps I, frankly, was absolutely amazed as the wickets fell.   It was the first time I had ever kept wicket to Appleyard.   He was faster than I had expected and his variety of pace as the ball swung through the air, made him most deceptive.   It is rather difficult to explain, but when he bowled Waqar Hassan, the ball appeared to be a half-volley just on the leg stump.   Waqar made to hit it away to mid-wicket, but the ball seemed to swing a little away from him and Waqar had played his shot before the ball arrived.   In other words the bat had gone through the shot just that fraction too soon, due to the deceptive swing, and the ball hit the off stump.   It was amazing how Bob Appleyard had those Pakistanis absolutely all at sea, although one must admit that they had not seen him before, and, in consequence, he was in full control of the situation.

Eventually, with the help of Alec Bedser and Johnny Wardle, we managed to bowl them out on that perfect Trent Bridge wicket for 157.   This was far better than we had hoped for, and made us fairly confident that we had the match in the bag, for we could not believe that the tourists could bowl us out for a small total on such a perfect wicket. Our hopes were fully justified.

After a slow start, David Sheppard and Reg Simpson got on top of the bowling and then proceeded to give it some hammer. We lost our first wicket—David's—when we were just two short of a hundred, and although Peter May, going in first wicket down, was immediately bowled by Khan, the tourists' delight did not last long. In came Denis Compton, and his arrival spelt trouble for the bowlers.

Denis was in his absolute peak form, and in one of his finest Test innings he reached 278, his highest Test score. The innings was not without its blemishes, however. He was missed off Fazal when he had scored 20 ; he made one or two errors after the 80's, and when he passed his 100, he took a few chances, dashing down the wicket in such a way that he gave those of us watching a few breath-catching moments. But in such a grand innings of run-getting at a fast pace, one is expected to have the occasional stroke of luck. That's cricket !

It was grand to see England's batsman in such fine form. Reg scored 101, eventually getting out off rather a bad shot—but after hitting a hundred, one could excuse him that. In any case, Tom Graveney followed, and he and Denis provided real fireworks, hitting at the rate of two runs a minute. Tom was his elegant self, and when he is in this form, there is nobody in the world who looks as good. He really did play a magnificent innings, and although he was eventually out for 84, we were in such a commanding position that it did not really matter.

David Sheppard declared at 558 for 6 and now it was a matter of how long the Pakistanis could stay. I'm afraid they didn't stay too long, and we won quite comfortably by an innings, although not before we had had a few shocks.

Little Hanif Mahommad was again a stumbling-block, as at Lord's. As you may know he is only a very small chap, but what a defensive player. He batted a very long time for his 51 in the second innings, and held us up for some considerable time. Then, of course, there was

Maqsood Ahmed. He was possibly the tourists' best stroke player, although he never really showed his true form, except in this innings. He got 69 and considering that he seemed in full command of the attack, I could not understand why he threw his wicket away as he did. When I say " he threw his wicket away ", I do not mean that he deliberately got himself out, for he was obviously trying to score runs all the time—but taking too many risks in so doing. Maqsood scored his 69 in just over the hour, which is fast scoring, but, actually, the batsmen should have been trying to save the match. Of course, Maqsood is a natural hitter of the ball, and times his shots well, but his impetuosity nearly ended his innings early on.

He hit one ball from Appleyard very hard and high to deep mid-wicket. It went to Brian Statham out in the deep and he missed it, the ball going for six. It is not very often that Statham misses a catch, but this was not an easy one, and even the best and safest of catchers drop one sometimes. However, Brian had his revenge. Later on, Maqsood hit a really terrific shot that went so high, it almost had ice on it when it came down. But this time, Brian, standing only a yard inside the boundary, got right under it and took a very brilliant catch. It was an unfortunate end to an adventurous innings, but Maqsood showed us that he had some great qualities as a run-getter.

With our bowlers sharing the wickets, (Bedser 2 ; Statham 3 ; Appleyard 2 ; and Wardle 3) we bowled Pakistan out for 272, to give us a comfortable victory. Summing up, I thought that Skipper Kardar was a trifle unfair to Khalid Hassan, the young leg-spin bowler. As far as I could see, he did not allow him to place his field as he wanted it, and certainly left so many gaps that Denis, Tom Graveney and most of the batsmen could score off this young lad at will, simply because the field was not set in the correct manner for this type of leg-spin bowler. At least, that was the opinion of those of us in the pavilion.

You see, Khalid doesn't spin it a lot but tosses it up and is quite accurate, and any cricketer knows that an accurate leg-spinner can set a field with confidence. Of course, we all know how difficult it is to bowl to a length —or even to a set field—when Denis is in form because he plays such fantastic shots. However, I do feel in my own mind that Kardar was harsh on this promising youngster (a) for bringing him in on the notorious Nottingham wicket, and (b) for not allowing him to set a correct field. It must have been disheartening to Khalid, making his Test debut.

Of the other Pakistanis, we realised once again what a fine opening batsman they had in Hanif Mohammad. Fazal Mahmood, unfortunately, pulled a muscle during the match and, therefore, could only bowl at half pace, but one had to admire his spirit, for he kept going when runs were coming so freely, and although he did not capture any wickets, he was unlucky, having one or two catches missed off him. He did enough, however, to prove to us that he would cause us plenty of trouble in future Tests.

It is perhaps a little unkind to criticise the batsmen, but it was obvious to all of us that they played the wrong game against Bob Appleyard. If they had played straighter and forward, going out to meet the ball more with the left foot down the wicket, I think they would have fared better than they did. They played him from the crease, with defensive back strokes which allowed the ball time to move off the pitch. Consequently, with Bob's deceptive change of pace, their defensive approach to their strokes got them into trouble.

Following our victory at Trent Bridge, we were in a pretty sound position when we went to Manchester, so in view of the tour to Australia the following winter, and the necessity to produce one or two youngsters for that trip, it came as no surprise when the selectors made further changes for the Old Trafford Test. David Sheppard was again captain, Len still not being very fit, while young Jim Parks, of Sussex, following in the footsteps of his father, came in for Reg Simpson, and Jim McConnon, off-spinner from Glamorgan, for Bob Appleyard.

Well, Manchester lived up to its " notorious " reputation, and play was restricted to little more than ten hours. This proved a further misfortune to our visitors, for this time the rain favoured England, although it must be admitted that the rain came at a time when Pakistan had virtually no chance of recovering from certain defeat. In consequence, the match was a draw.

Running quickly through the match, David Sheppard won the toss, and decided to bat on a goodish wicket. After a reasonable start, Trevor Bailey opening with the skipper, Denis was again in magnificent form. Once more, he and Tom Graveney were the backbone of our batting, scoring 93 and 65 respectively. Jim Parks opened quite smartly and was batting very well until, trying to play a leg glide off Fazal, he was bowled around his legs and had his leg stump knocked down. Still, we had seen enough of Jim to know that the promise was there. I managed to collect 31, and then Johnny Wardle came in and began to enjoy himself with a merry 54.

What an entertaining chap he is. When he is batting no one quite knows what he is going to do, for he can play defensively and very correctly when the occasion demands, yet on another occasion he leaps down the wicket and hits the ball a tremendous wallop. I should think that Johnny hits the ball harder and further than anybody playing today when he really middles it. On this occasion he certainly middled one or two, and hit three beautiful sixes. One of them completely cleared the Old Trafford ground. No wonder the crowds love him !

Pakistan brought in their left-arm bowler Shujauddin, and he came in for some real hammer from Johnny Wardle. " Shuja " had a strange, jerky action, and I remember sitting up in the dressing-room watching him. Every time he ran up to bowl, there was a chorus of " Hup-hup-hoy ! " in time with his uncommon action. Then, as he delivered the ball, up would go our arms to signal " six ". Johnny hit him for three gigantic sixes

At Tower Isle Hotel, in Jamaica, one of the popular tourist seaside resorts, members of the M.C.C. team listening to a calypso composed in their honour. On the table can be seen a cake topped by a cricket pitch in icing, presented to the team by Mr. Arthur Collier, manager of the Tower Isle Hotel, and formerly at the Savoy (London). The players are *(left to right)* : Trevor Bailey, Willie Watson, Tom Graveney, Johnny Wardle, Len Hutton, Godfrey Evans, Jim Laker and Dick Spooner.

In British Guiana, mounted police patrol the cricket ground during the matches. Godfrey Evans, himself a keen horseman in his younger days, decided to give one of the police horses some exercise, and Willie Watson (Yorkshire) took this photograph of him prior to a canter round the playing pitch.

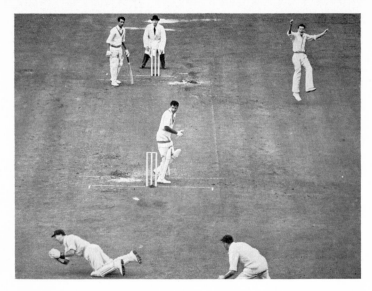

The Oval, 1954—the author equals Bertie Oldfield's world record with his
130th Test victim.   Fazal Mahmood got an inside edge off Peter Loader, who is
seen appealing, with the Pakistan captain, A. H. Kardar, looking on.   Incidentally, later in the same innings, Godfrey Evans passed the previous record when
he caught Kardar off Brian Statham.

The author and Len Hutton chatting with the Captain of the s.s. *Orsova* on the
day of the M.C.C.'s departure to Australia in 1954.   In the background are
Colin Cowdrey, Tom Graveney and Alec Bedser.

During the match against the Combined XI, at Perth (1954–55), Graham Hole attempted a second run to Tom Graveney, fielding at third man. A good throw, and the author had the bails off with the Australian batsman out of his ground. The umpire's decision of " Not out " came as rather a surprise—as the above photograph proves.

Golfing, at Perth, Western Australia, during off-duty hours. *Left to right :* Len Hutton, the Governor of Western Australia, Tom Graveney and the author, returning from a round on the Royal Perth Links.

The M.C.C. party that brought back the Ashes from Australia (1954–55). *Left to right :* (*back row*) G. Duckworth (Baggage-master and scorer), Andrew, Loader, Graveney, Tyson, H. W. Dalton (Masseur) ; (*middle row*) Wardle, Simpson, Wilson, Appleyard, McConnon, Statham, Cowdrey, Mr. Howard (Manager) ; (*front row*) Bailey, Edrich, May, Hutton, Compton, and I suppose we expected more. Please don't imagine that I am trying to ridicule " Shuja ". Far from it. He's a cheerful sort of a chap and by no means a bad bowler. It just happened that he came in for punishment because we were well on top, and Johnny Wardle was having a go. He proved a very useful left-arm bowler during the tour and this last winter, against the New Zealanders, he has been well among the wickets.

When David Sheppard declared we were 359 for 8, and then it was our turn to perform in the field. As I have told you, we were in luck. After heavy rain, the wicket was rather difficult. Yet even this had its compensation, in a way, because we wanted to see how Jim McConnon bowled, and fielded close to the wicket. We were not disappointed, for Jim captured 3 wickets for 19 in 13 overs, which was not at all a bad performance, and he took three good catches. I was very impressed with his close-to-the-wicket fielding, for he moved quickly and took his catches well. He might have had two more ; Jim got his hands to them even though they were travelling very fast off the edge of the bat, but he could not quite hold them long enough. I am sure his performance at Old Trafford clinched his place in the Australian tour.

We bowled Pakistan out for 90 and made them follow on, and they finished up with 25 for 4 in the second innings. You can see from that how we were well on top, and unquestionably the better side. However, rain had left the rubber still open, for with a bit of luck, Pakistan could draw the series with a victory in the Fourth and final Test, although I am quite certain that no one expected them to do this on their first visit to England. Yet they surprised us all. They won a close, well-fought game at the Oval by 24 runs.

England really had the worst of the wicket, but that is no excuse. It was our own fault for not taking advantage of the time when we had a good chance to do so. The primary reason why we lost was the brilliant bowling of Fazal Mahmood, who took 6 wickets in each innings. It was a great performance considering that at one stage it looked as if we were odds on favourites to win by a comfortable margin.

Bailey and Bedser were rested for this Test in favour of Frank Tyson and Peter Loader, both making their Test debut. So with Tyson, Statham and Loader we had a very fast attack, and it did not take them long to get cracking. In fact they took the wickets between them—Tyson 4, Loader 3 and Statham 2. Frank Tyson impressed me from the start. It was my first opportunity of keeping wicket to him, and although the wicket was rather sluggish, he came through very quickly. I was standing back a fair way, but I had to move very quickly to get to the ball.

We bowled Pakistan out for 133 but then the rain came, and they bowled us out for 130, which gave them an even chance in the second innings. Len Hutton was back but did not get going ; Reg Simpson was out early on ; Denis and Peter May played some good shots and put up a stand for a time ; but then Fazal hit his form, and the wickets tumbled. He finished with 6 wickets and nobody in the last half-dozen batsmen made double figures, except Jim McConnon who got 11.

We had a rather long tail, but then if the recognised batsmen don't get runs, it is hardly likely that the tail-enders will be able to—at least, not in the normal run of things, and seldom in Test cricket. However, we failed, so that was that.

Now for the second innings, and with the wicket as it was, we felt we had a reasonable chance of bowling Pakistan out for a cheap score, for we had Johnny Wardle, and Jim McConnon. If they used the wicket properly, we had a good chance.

David soon took off his fast bowlers and Johnny and Jim took over, but the result was not quite what we expected. I'm afraid Jim McConnon did not strike his best form, yet I feel sure that if only he had been bowling as we knew he could, and had struck a length, he would have got five or six wickets. On the other hand, Johnny Wardle took 7 for 56 in 35 overs. It was a good performance, but it was not Johnny at his best. Anyway, Pakistan scored 164 when, to my mind, they should have been bowled out for 50.

It was rather disheartening to see this wicket that should have been such a help to our bowlers wasted, and those bowlers being hit when they should have been getting wickets. Jim was turning the ball all right, and it was a nasty wicket to bat on but if the ball is not dropped on a length on such wickets, it proves a disadvantage to the bowler and a great advantage to the batsman. On rain-affected wickets a bowler must definitely be more accurate than he needs to be on a very hard wicket, because the margin of error is so much smaller. If the ball is pitched say a foot shorter than it should be, it lifts, and the batsman has more time to get back and crack it round the corner, or wherever he wants it to go.

On the other hand, if the wicket is hard and the ball pitches a foot shorter than it should, it skids through on to the bat and is too quick for the batsman to get in position for a forcing shot, but if it is well up, then the batsman has time to go down and crack it full toss before it pitches and does its work. So it must always be remembered that on difficult wickets batsmen sometimes score unexpected runs because of bad bowling—or, shall we say, incorrect bowling. I think this was partly the case in this Oval Test.

During the innings I spoke to Jim and tried to encourage him, for I could see that he was a little disappointed. He shrugged and said: " I'm sorry, I've just lost it for the moment." Maybe it was Test match nerves, but whatever it was, we knew this was not the real Jim McConnon.

I repeat, we should definitely have bowled Pakistan out for a much smaller score than 164, yet even with that score, I still think we should have won. After all, the wicket had bucked up, and we needed only 168 to win. It did not seem beyond us, and with more than 2½ hours before close of play on the fourth day, the policy was to go for the runs and try to finish it that evening, so that we would have a day to spare. Every cricketer likes a day's holiday, you know, and we knew that Pakistan were not really strong in bowling, except for Fazal Mahmood.

As it happened, this desire for quick runs was our own undoing. We tried, and we failed. I went in before Tom Graveney when we were 115 for 4. By now we felt we were nearly there, for we needed only another 53 and still had 6 wickets to go. I remember Len saying to me :

" Do you fancy going in and scoring a few quickly so that we can get it over tonight in case of rain tomorrow ? "

I replied—and meant it : " Certainly, Skipper, I'll do what I can."

Well, the first ball, just short of a length from Fazal, bit into the rain-affected pitch turf and whistled past my nose. I just had time to draw my head out of the way ! That surprised me and Denis Compton at the other end said : " It's not so easy as it looks from the circle, is it ? " It certainly wasn't easy, and I did not last long. Denis and Tom also followed me before close of play that evening.

We were in real trouble now, for when play began next morning we had only 3 wickets left and still had some way to go for the runs we needed. What is more, Fazal was in top form. He soon had Frank Tyson out. Jim McConnon was run out off of a very slick piece of fielding, and eventually Johnny Wardle was caught off Fazal to finish the match. Thus we lost by 24 runs. All praise to Pakistan for their fight back, because when we were standing at 115 for 4 it certainly looked odds on our victory. However, it was a great tribute to them that they had drawn the series in their first Test rubber in England.

On the whole, I would say they were lucky to draw the series because England were definitely the better side, but they took every advantage of the situation, while I'm afraid it must be admitted that we underestimated them. Yet I am sure that tour did a great deal for Pakistan cricket in general. I have heard that boys all over Pakistan are now trying to bowl like Fazal Mahmood, the hero of that historic Oval Test, and trying to bat like Hanif Mohammad. If all the youngsters in the country take those two grand cricketers as their examples, then I am sure many fine young players will come out of Pakistan in the future to mark their name on the international roll of cricket.

So ended a series that was rather spoilt by the bad weather. It really was a very bad summer indeed, and we were all very glad when the season finished.

Before I pass on to other subjects, however, I must record that this final Test at the Oval was one I shall always remember. When I caught Fazal off Peter Loader in the second innings, I obtained my 130th victim behind the stumps, thus equalling Bertie Oldfield's world record. A few overs later I beat the record when I caught Kardar off Brian Statham. That was a great day for me.

Records must play a part in cricket, although I hold the opinion that, unlike athletics for instance, a cricketer should never go out to attempt to break a record, unless it is in the full interest of the team. Yet, there is no doubt at all that when a record *is* surpassed, it brings a thrill of pride to the record holder. That is human nature. So you can be sure I was very proud when I captured the world's record of 131 victims behind the stumps. Such a record does not mean anything really, but I suppose when my cricketing days are over, I shall look back with nostalgic memories to that catch off Brian Statham.

It gave me a tremendous amount of pleasure, for, after all, I suppose we are all prone to feel proud of a special achievement. Life is a constant search for achievement —and the desire to do something better than anyone else —or something that no one else has done. It makes life worthwhile.

There is just one other point about this business of breaking cricket records. So far as I am concerned, anything I can do well is a credit to my County, Kent—and to England, especially if it is a Test record.

CHAPTER VIII

The Ashes Retained—1954–55

WITH THE ASHES IN OUR POSSESSION WE LOOKED FORWARD
to the next trip to Australia with considerable
optimism and with the determination to hold on to them.
I can honestly say that I had never experienced such an
optimistic spirit in any M.C.C. touring party of which I
had been a member. We felt we had the measure of the
Australians, and that having beaten them once, we could
do it again—in their own country.

Len Hutton, the man who had led us to victory in that
memorable Oval Test when England regained the Ashes
for the first time since 1932, was rightly given the captaincy of the touring party, although not without some
criticism, as I explain in a later chapter.

The decision to take a party of 18 players on the tour
was received with mixed comments, but I believe I am
right in saying that it was Len Hutton himself who was
responsible for increasing the normal touring party.
For one thing, there was a doubt about Denis Compton,
for, you will remember, he could not join the party for
the voyage as he was still undergoing treatment to his
knee. Arrangements were made for him to fly out a
few weeks after our arrival—providing no complication
developed.

Then again, no doubt Len remembered our experience
in 1950–51 under Freddie Brown, when we had to send
for Brian Statham and Roy Tattersall because of illness
and injuries to members of the touring party. They flew
out direct from an English winter into the Australian heat,
and, without adequate practice, had to try to acclimatise
themselves in actual match play.

In view of this, I think I can understand Len's reason-
ing in advocating 18 instead of the usual 16 players.

Few touring teams avoid injury to one or two players.
It had happened to us before and Len evidently believed
that in such circumstances it was better to have men on
the spot, fully acclimatised and ready to step in, than to
send for replacements, as had happened with Statham
and Tattersall.

In this connection, I think it would be an excellent idea
if, in future, when 16 players are chosen to tour, three or
four others were paid to stand by and keep match fit
throughout the winter so that, in dire emergency, those
needed could be flown direct to join the depleted touring
party and be ready for immediate duty in the team.

On this occasion, however, the experiment was tried
of taking 18 players—in case of necessity. Len can
hardly be blamed because that necessity did not arise and
the experiment failed. The team suffered only a minimum amount of injury and, in consequence, it was difficult
to give all 18 players enough match play to keep everybody
in top form. This was particularly noticeable so far as
the batting was concerned.

Some of our leading batsmen were slow in hitting their
true form, while others were a success from the start.
This proved a problem. Should the men in form be
dropped so that others could be given the chance to play
themselves into form—or should the successful batsmen
be given precedence, thus preventing the others getting
sufficient match practice ?   Yes, it was indeed a problem,
but as events turned out, Len solved it as well as he could,
and I feel that the team did not suffer unduly, although
there is no doubt that it affected some individual players.

So far as the team selections were concerned, there was
considerable bewilderment among most of us as to why
Willie Watson was not in the side. After all, the Yorkshire " double international " did a magnificent job in
the West Indies on the previous tour both as left-handed
batsman—he scored one 200 and three 100's on the tour—
and a brilliant outfielder. Being an international foot-
baller, Willie is very quick off the mark and stops those
hard drives at cover better than anyone else I know.

I could not understand Vic Wilson being selected in his place. I should be the last person to criticise our selectors, but I personally could see no reason at all for choosing a hitherto untried Yorkshireman—untried as a Test player of course—when in Willie Watson we had a cricketer of great ability, and one, moreover, who had proved his worth. I believe that Len Hutton and Norman Yardley felt that Vic Wilson, with his physique and temperament, would be able to tame the fast attack of Lindwall and Miller. Unfortunately, though a grand tourist, Vic never got going with the bat, though his general fielding and close-to-the-wicket catching helped us to many a victory, and he was twelfth man in every Test.

My most outstanding memory of the outward boat trip was passing through Suez. If you remember, at that particular time the British troops in the Canal Zone were having a pretty tough time, but as we moved slowly through the Canal, there were the boys lining the banks, their band playing. We were allowed up on the Captain's bridge, and answered the frantic cheering of the troops. It was an inspiring and memorable moment for all of us.

At Suez an officer came aboard with a tape machine and we recorded messages so that they could be played back to the troops. Colin Cowdrey and I sent our good wishes and news from home to the boys of Kent, while Len Hutton, Johnny Wardle, Bob Appleyard and Vic Wilson addressed the boys of Yorkshire, and so on right through the whole team. We heard afterwards how much the troops appreciated that act, but they could not have enjoyed it any more than we did. I shall never forget looking out from the ship's bridge and seeing the bronzed Canal Zone troops lined along the banks and cheering as wildly as though we had already won the Test series.

When we arrived in Colombo I looked forward to seeing for the first time Frank Tyson cracking them down on really hard wickets. The only time I had kept wicket to him was in the last Test for England against Pakistan a few weeks previously. However, that was a soft wicket, but even then I found him very quick, so I was quite certain he would be considerably quicker when he got going on hard wickets. Unfortunately, I was not fit to play in our one-day match because of my damaged finger, but I watched Keith Andrew keep to his Northants colleague, and noted with some interest the tremendous distance he had to stand back behind the stumps to Frank's pace and also to Brian Statham. It made me think !

That " pipe-opener " at Colombo proved to us that we definitely had some real pace in our attack, but it was not until we got to Perth that I had a chance to try out the speed of Frank and Brian, by keeping to them. (I've seen plenty of them since !)

It was at Perth that we got our land legs and began to settle down. First of all the team selectors were appointed, and I felt very proud to be chosen to join Len, Peter May, Bill Edrich and Mr. Howard, our manager. It was my second association with Len on an M.C.C. Selection Committee, for I had that honour under Skipper Freddie Brown on the previous Australian tour.

Len proved himself a grand skipper during those early days in Perth, when we were all trying to acclimatise ourselves in the nets. This is always exhausting for the bowlers, for remember, everybody wants to have a knock, which means that the bowlers get precious little rest. To make matters even more difficult, we had no legspinners in our party—Jim McCannon was an off-spinner, Johnnie Wardle a left-armer, and Bob Appleyard a rather fastish off-spinner.

So Len invited two of the visiting English Pressmen to bowl to us at the nets—none other than former England skipper Freddie Brown, and ex-Test player Ian Peebles. They willingly agreed to swing the arm over, which not only gave our bowlers a brief rest in between their spells at the nets, but it gave us a little practice against leg-spin bowling. This was most invaluable, as we were due to come up against that type of attack from Richie Benaud and others when the tour started in earnest.

8

We owed quite a lot to Freddie and Ian—but then I know they enjoyed helping us out.

We had one serious set-back early on in the tour. On the boat going out, Alec Bedser complained of an ache around his shoulder, but it was not until he started loosening up in Perth, that he found the trouble was more serious than he thought. Alec came out in a rash all round his bowling arm, a very nasty rash, too, and the doctor diagnosed shingles.

I remember calling on Alec when he had been sent to bed, and poor Alec was looking very fed-up.

" I thought shingles was caused by worry and nerves," I said to him.

" That's what the doctor says," Alec replied, " but I can't understand it. I have nothing to worry about. I've had a jolly good benefit, I didn't go on tour last winter because I wanted a good rest, and I was really looking forward to this tour. I just can't understand it, but there it is."

It was bad luck for Alec, for I am sure that serious dose of shingles unsettled him and robbed us of his bowling in most of the Test matches. Still it was just one of those things that happen and we could do nothing about it.

At last we got down to serious cricket and played two matches at Perth—against Western Australia and a Combined XI. I was then fit again so I played in both games for I was eager to keep wicket to Frank Tyson, with his terrific pace, and Brian Statham, who had improved so much since his first short visit to Australia that he was now a really great fast bowler.

By the way, did you know that Brian's shoulders are double jointed ? He can clasp his hands behind his back and bring them to the front over his head without letting go. If you care to try that you will find it most difficult. Some of Brian's tricks have to be seen to be believed. He kept us in fits of laughter at times. I have seen him put his right arm at the back of his head and bring his right hand right round to the left of his face, under the chin and tickle his right ear. If you don't think that is difficult, try it yourself! Then attempt it with both hands—as Brian does. Well, I couldn't do it—could you?

But to return to the cricket. It was during those two matches at Perth that I thought the writing was on the wall for Australia. In other words, I saw enough in those games to feel assured that we had the beating of the Australians. In the Combined XI were Ian Johnson, Neil Harvey and Graham Hole, who were flown thousands of miles to play. It was hoped that they would strengthen the side and also give them some practice against our pace. In actual fact, these three great Test stars made very few runs, and were frankly disappointing, so their trip proved a somewhat expensive experiment.

The wickets in Perth are fast, there is no question about it. On each of my Australian tours Perth has provided the fastest wickets of the whole trip and these were no exception. Certainly they gave every chance to our bowlers to show their pace. The Australians were in trouble right away, in fact, Neil Harvey could not get going at all. I caught him in both innings behind the wicket because the ball was coming through much faster than he expected.

Graham Hole fared little better. He is an elegant player when he gets going, but with his high flowing back lift, the ball is inclined to get through before his bat comes down, and against our pace-men on that Perth wicket this proved fatal.

But if Graham and Neil failed with the bat, at least we were given a chance to see Ian Johnson bowling once again, for remember he had been out of favour with the Australian Board of Control, and did not come to England in the 1953 tour. On this occasion he bowled with that same deceptive flight that gained him so many wickets on our previous tour. All we players contend that Ian throws, although no Australian would agree, and as he passes muster with the umpires, perhaps it is a matter of opinion ; but with his bent elbow action, it enables him to deceive the batsman and make the ball drop shorter than the average bowler of his type. Again, with a bent elbow he seems to be able to impart a deceptive spin on the ball. Whether it is because the ball drops fast and then gets the spin off the wicket I really cannot say, but it seems to pay him dividends, judging from the wickets he takes.

After Ian Johnson's performance against us at Perth, it looked as though he was going to regain his place in the Test side. If that was so, we assumed that he would be in the running for captaincy. We were right as it turned out, but before we continue with our story of the tour just a word about this question of captaincy.

The Australians choose their captain in a peculiar way —peculiar, that is, to our method. A certain body of selectors pick the Test team, and from their selections a name is put forward for captain to another Board. If that name is acceptable, the selection is confirmed, but if not, then the Board can select their own captain.

In the latter case, the majority of votes goes to the major State side, which is Victoria. I think there are 12 votes in all—2 from Queensland, 2 from South Australia, 1 from Western Australia, 3 from New South Wales, and the remainder—the majority of 4—from Victoria. So you see, if it comes to a vote, and Queensland side up with Victoria, then they have a majority over the others right away, unless, of course, two or three of the others vote with New South Wales. That is why it so seldom happens that Australia choose a captain from any but the two major States. I know that Sir Donald Bradman was selected when he was with South Australia, but that was an exception.

Anyway, with Ian Johnson back in form—and favour —it was quite obvious to us, even thus early in the tour, that the Test captaincy would rest between Ian Johnson and Arthur Morris of New South Wales.

From Perth we moved on to Adelaide, and it was there that we were joined by Denis Compton. Only a couple of days after stepping off the plane, he was put in against South Australia and, to the delight of the whole party, he hit a grand hundred. The people of Adelaide expected something extra-special from him, and he did not disappoint them—or us. But that is one of Denis' assets ; he has the natural aptitude to rise to the occasion when the occasion demands something from him.

It was a wonderful performance, especially when you remember that Denis had had a rather unnerving experience on the flight out. As the plane came in to land at Karachi, the undercarriage mechanism jammed, and the pilot had to make a belly landing. Fortunately there were no injuries, although it must have given Denis a shake-up.

After the two games in Perth, several of us were rested for the Adelaide match, so Mr. Howard and Len Hutton allowed those of us who were not playing in Adelaide to travel to Melbourne, where we would play our next game, so that we could see the famous and fabulous Melbourne Cup.

Melbourne Cup Day is absolutely terrific, resembling Ascot or the Derby. The weather was changeable, but, fortunately, the favourite, " Rising Fast ", justified everyone's hopes, and as most of the boys were on it, we made a small profit on the day. So our trip was well worth while, and most enjoyable, too.

Our match at Melbourne against an Australian XI was rain affected, which was a great pity, for we were now beginning to settle down, and form was sorting itself out.

That Melbourne match was also Alec Bedser's first appearance of the tour, following his attack of shingles, and we were all anxious to know how much the lay-off would affect his bowling. As we had two more matches before the first Test, it was essential that Alec was given as much preparation as possible. In actual fact, of course, he started a bit too soon and it affected him for the remainder of the tour. No blame was attached to anyone. Alec was keen to get back into harness, and none of us could foresee just what would happen.

When we played at Melbourne, we were beginning to form some idea of our probable team for the first Test, although there were still a few problems, especially among the batsmen. Reg Simpson, for instance, one of the world's greatest stroke players, batted beautifully for an hour and then got himself out to a very careless shot. Reg is inclined to be a little moody—call it temperamental if you like—and if he does not feel quite up to it, he sometimes takes chances at the wicket which cause his downfall.

The same applies to Tom Graveney. When he is in the mood, there are few better stroke players. But during the early part of the tour he would make twenty or thirty beautiful runs, and then get himself out through lack of concentration, resulting in a foolish shot. It was most disconcerting, for we knew that Tom should have been making his hundreds.

The bowling was also presenting problems. The pacemen were taking most of the wickets, and for that reason, the spinners were not getting much opportunity to show results. Take Johnnie Wardle for example. He had few chances in the previous matches and although he did not bowl at all badly when he was called upon, he did not get among the wickets.

Bob Appleyard certainly took a few wickets in his early games, but I feel that he was then trying to bowl too fast. It must be said in his favour that the warm climate suited him, and he admitted he had not felt so well for years, and for that reason he seemed to let himself go. But that made him, virtually, another medium pacer, instead of a spinner, which, of course, was what we lacked.

Jim McConnon, our other spinner, could not strike the form that had made him so successful during the previous home season, and, in consequence, our spin attack looked decidedly thin.

That Melbourne match did little to ease our problem in this respect. Nor did the next game, against New South Wales, at Sydney, where Keith Miller, to my mind the greatest all-rounder in post-war cricket, was captaining the State side. Yet that match certainly solved one of our problems.

Until then, my young Kent colleague, Colin Cowdrey, had not really revealed the form of which we knew he was capable, yet at Sydney he more than earned his place in the team for the first Test. He hit a hundred in each innings.

I was really thrilled to be batting at the other end when he made the first of those two centuries. I was there again when he was going strongly in the second innings, but I am afraid I was out while he was still in the nineties, much to my disappointment.

Up to this time as I have said already, we were a trifle worried about our early batting, particularly the openers. As an experiment, Len Hutton decided to give Colin the onerous task of opening our second innings, and his brilliant display, bringing him his second hundred of the match, gave us hope that we had found a worthy opener.

So Colin was chosen as opening partner to Reg Simpson for our next match at Brisbane, against Queensland, but perhaps this was a little unfair to him. It meant that Colin had to face the opening overs of Ray Lindwall, and that is asking a lot of any young batsman ! It was not his lucky day and he failed in both innings. But that could have happened to even the greatest of openers, for Ray Lindwall was then—and still is—the greatest new ball bowler in the world. Maybe Ray is not quite so fast as he used to be, but he still keeps the ball well up to the bat.

However, it meant that Colin had failed as an opening batsman. It was disappointing, for we were hoping so much that he would partner Len Hutton in the Tests and solve our problem.

During the New South Wales match, at Sydney, many of us saw the young Australian fast bowler, Pat Crawford, for the first time. He quite impressed us and got among our wickets. Since then he has been over to England to play with success in the Lancashire League, and no doubt he has learnt a lot about English weather and wickets. I feel he might cause us quite a lot of trouble in the future. He bowls from a longish run, he is rather tall, perhaps on the slim side (a little lanky, as we would say), but when he delivers the ball he puts his whole body weight behind his arm.

Keith Miller was telling me that Pat never gives up. Even when Keith has wanted to take him off, Pat has pleaded : " Let me have another over or so." I admire that spirit, especially in a young fast bowler. It is one of the fundamentals of cricket success. We could do with more of it.

By the way, while we were in Sydney, we met our old friend John Human, who used to play for Middlesex. He went on an M.C.C. tour, way back before the war, married an Australian girl, and now has a nice house in Sydney and another in Palm Beach.

On each of my visits to Australia, John has invited the whole M.C.C. party to his " Beach House " for an open barbecue and to go swimming at Palm Beach. (Wonderful thought !) The last time we were there he took us out on a friend's yacht for a trip up the Hawkesbury River. It was a grand break from cricket.

From Sydney we moved on to Brisbane for our fixture with Queensland, prior to the first Test.

Now Brisbane does not hold particularly happy memories for me. When I was there in 1946 with Wally Hammond's team, I was not chosen for the first Test. Paul Gibb kept wicket. Then in 1950–51, with Freddie Brown's side, rain robbed us of whatever chance we had of victory, and on this last tour, my Brisbane " hoodoo " again reared its head. I had a bad bout of flu and I had to listen in to the first two days of the Test match lying in bed. You can be sure that didn't please me—especially in view of the team's disappointing start, but more of that later.

I was not playing in the match against Queensland that preceded the Test, either, so I was able to watch points. The wicket was certainly very different from that prepared for the Test—there was some life in it. But what really mattered now was the choice of the Test team, and here was our last chance to decide on our attack. It presented problems.

Should we rely on an all-pace attack ? Should we choose the spinners ? And what of Alec Bedser ? It was generally felt that Alec should play because of the psychological effect on the opposition, but had he recovered sufficiently ? Yes, it was a problem.

Frank Tyson had proved himself with his pace and he was getting more accurate with every match. Brian Statham was obviously a safe bet, too. But what of the others ?

Trevor Bailey had been doing well with both bat and ball throughout the tour, while Bob Appleyard was striving hard to recover his true form, although I still contend that he was trying to bowl too fast. He was virtually, therefore, another seamer, and I thought Alec Bedser could do his job just as well. Then there was Johnny Wardle, who had not taken a wicket since Perth, although one must admit that he had few opportunities. But could we take a risk ?

It was very difficult for us to make up our minds, but after much deliberation we decided to plump for Alec and Trevor to support the fast attack of Tyson and Statham, and depending on Denis Compton to bowl his spinners should the wicket prove difficult. Denis is by no means a bad bowler. In actual fact, in Test cricket I think he has taken about 48 wickets, which is no mean feat.

When I left the Selection Committee meeting with Bill Edrich we met Trevor Bailey in the lift.

" Well, what's the side, boys ? " Trevor asked.

When we told him, he said : " I don't like the look of that ! I'm going to get myself a large whisky without much water ! "

I am afraid Trevor misinterpreted the reasons for the selections we had made. He pointed out that the last time England had played four fast bowlers in a Test side at Melbourne in 1932, on a wicket that was made for spinners, we lost. Trevor seemed to think that we should encounter the same trouble this time, and, as events proved, he was right, but let me assure you that Len, Peter, Bill and I were convinced at the time that we were making the right selections, in view of the fact that our spinners had not really proved themselves.

As a player of considerable experience, Trevor's opinions naturally carried some weight with other members of the party who were inclined to agree with him, and, in consequence, the team spirit was not as whole-hearted as it might have been.

Now although I did not play in the Brisbane Test, I am sure that the half-hearted attitude that seemed to pervade the whole team was partly responsible for the poor fielding and the spate of dropped catches that enabled the Australians to put up such a mammoth score, and win easily by more than an innings.

It is easy to be wise after the event, yet on reflection I think we were wrong in not playing a genuine spinner, but we had agreed on our policy of a speed attack, and we accepted the responsibility for the disappointing result.

Having lost the first Test, our next task was to find a team for the Sydney Test. We were all certain that we had the players to beat Australia. The result of the first Test was unfortunate, but it was obvious that the boys could do better—much better. I am sure that the undercurrent of tension in the side had much to do with our defeat. However, things weren't really so bad as they appeared, despite the criticism some of our selections received.

For instance, many people, both at home and in Australia, wanted to know why we included Edrich. Well, although Bill had failed with the bat in the early games, we all knew his fighting qualities in Test cricket—and Bill did not fail us. His 88 in the second innings proved that we were right in choosing him.

Tom Graveney had stomach trouble, so he was out, and, remember, Denis Compton broke a bone in his hand in the first hour of play, so he was virtually out, too. All the other batsmen failed, except for Trevor Bailey. He was well on the way to his first century of the tour, and wanted only twelve more, when he tried to hit Bill Johnston out of the ground and had his castle knocked over. But he did play well. Trevor is not perhaps a really great batsman, but he seems to find some extra ability when the occasion demands on Test fields.

With Trevor—not one of our recognised batsmen, remember—scoring 88 and Bill equalling that score when out of form, I think we were justified in the hope that we could settle down and, in the next Test, score enough runs to give our attack a chance to put us on the winning trail. That was our next problem.

Meanwhile, however, with the first Test over, we were due to fulfil a fixture at Rockhampton which is on the tropical side of Queensland. As I was still not too well, Len thought it better for me not to travel with the team, so four of the boys and I went back to Sydney and stayed at the Rose-Bay Golf Club, a really wonderful spot.

It is within a couple of miles of the centre of Sydney, with a beautiful club-house, and marvellous food. The four days we spent there, playing lots of golf and squash, were most enjoyable. That short break put me right back into peak fitness, so that when we went to Canberra to play a one-day match against the Prime Minister's XI I was feeling in the mood for cricket once more.

Just a word about Mr. Robert Menzies, " Our Bob ", as all Australians know him. He is a wonderful character, and he certainly made us feel very much at home. We visited his lodge and had a game of snooker with him. Lindsay Hassett and several of the Australian Test players were there, too, as members of the Prime Minister's side.

I recall one amusing incident during our visit. After a game of snooker and a very excellent meal, Lindsay Hassett was bragging about playing bouncers.

" You wait until I am batting against Tyson tomorrow," he said. " I'll show you how to hook his bouncer."

The following day, Lindsay Hassett came in to bat and it happened that Frank Tyson was bowling. As he passed Frank he said with a grin : " Now steady on, Frank, I didn't really mean what I said last night."

Frank laughed. " All right, Lindsay, I'll be careful,' he replied, and bowled him the gentlest of balls.

All went well until Frank suddenly called down the wicket : " It's coming this time, Lindsay, so watch out ! "

After such a warning, Lindsay knew he had to back up his boast of the previous evening.

Down came the ball, and by jove it *was* a quick one ! Lindsay only just managed to stop it from hitting him in the face.   When he recovered he looked down the wicket and said : " All right, Frank !   I take back what I said last night, so don't you bowl another of those at me ! "

It was all in good fun, of course, but I'm sure it made Lindsay think.   Not having faced Frank at his best, it must have made him realise that the Northants pace-man was quicker than the usual run of fast bowlers.

During the earlier part of the tour, and particularly at Brisbane, some of us felt that Frank Tyson was taking too much out of himself with his tremendous run in that hot climate, often under a blazing sun, but we hesitated to say anything, in case we put him off his form.   We felt that the best way to handle the situation with a bowler of Frank's temperament and type was to let him sort it out himself.   It was no good telling him to cut down his run straight away ;   much better to let him experiment.

At the start of the tour he had rather a shuffle for three or four paces, before leaping into longer strides until he reached his maximum pace at the point of delivery.   Most of us felt that a shorter run-up would not only enable him to gain his maximum pace more quickly, but would help him to conserve his stamina and energy for longer periods.

I think Frank himself realised that he could not sustain his pace and efficiency unless he did something about it and after a long chat with Len, Frank agreed to try a shortened run.   The experiment was an immediate success, and from then on the whole side seemed to click into gear.

Against Victoria the all-round improvement was obvious and we approached the second Test with greater optimism—and a few team changes.

This time we included Wardle and Appleyard, and Tom Graveney was in for Reg Simpson.   We didn't pick

Alec Bedser, and our decision brought criticism heaping down upon us not only from the English Press but also from the people of Australia. Alec is a very popular player indeed out there, both with the players and the spectators, but much as we disliked doing it, we had to bow to the inevitable. Alec was not his normal self at that time, not having fully recovered from his illness. We felt that it was unfair to such a big-hearted fellow as Alec to expect him to face the strain of a Sydney Test when he was in need of a rest. Better to give him a rest in Sydney and, if necessary, bring him back at Melbourne we contended.

Sydney greeted us with rain, and although the Test opened on time, when Arthur Morris won the toss for Australia, he decided to put us in. Quite right, too ! His decision was justified for we lost 4 wickets for 60. It seemed that we were in trouble again, but it is rather extraordinary how teams who bat first in Australia and fare only moderately, have a habit of overcoming the ordeal, recovering in the second innings and winning the match. It does not always occur, of course, but it has happened quite often. It happened this time. . . .

Our first innings score was not exactly a big one, but it might have been far worse had it not been for tail-enders Wardle and Statham. Johnny, who had not been making many runs, suddenly popped up out of the blue, and he and Brian put on 43 for the last wicket. We were right back in the game, and our tails were up.

I thought Trevor Bailey made a good job of opening the innings. Not that he scored many runs, but he played the sort of game which we have come to expect of him. In each innings he stayed long enough to see the shine off the new ball and give a better chance to the following batsmen, which they definitely took in our second innings, after we—or, at least, our pace attack—had put Australia out for 228.

Peter May and Colin Cowdrey took charge after we had lost 3 for 55, and put on over 100 together. Peter hit 104 and Colin got 54—two wonderful innings. No one was more delighted about their success than Len Hutton, who, earlier on in the tour, had been discussing players with Keith Miller. Keith boasted that Australia had the best young batsman in the world in Richie Benaud. Len wasn't having any of that, and he started to eulogise on the promise of Peter May.

" All right," said Keith, " I'll have a bet with you that Richie Benaud will make more runs than Peter May in the Tests."

Len readily took him on. Well, of course, events proved Len's prediction justified. Peter was a great success, but Richie was virtually a failure so far as his batting was concerned. Keith had to admit it, too. After the final Test he paid up his bet and sportingly confessed : " You were right, Len. Peter May and Colin Cowdrey are the two best young batsmen in the world today."

To return to the Sydney Test—praise once again was deserved by our last-wicket pair. In the first innings it was Statham and Wardle ; in the second Bob Appleyard came into his own, and he and Brian put on 46 for the last wicket.

By now the fight was really on. We had the runs on the board, and a lead of 222, and when we went out on the morning of the last day Australia still needed 151, with eight wickets standing. The odds were on Australia, but as we prepared to take the field, I remember saying : " Come on, boys ! We shall be there at the finish."

Brian and Frank opened the bowling, but not very successfully. For the first two overs the ball seemed to find the centre of the bat, and gave us no indication of the fireworks to come. For the first overs Frank did not work up his usual pace but then, with a strong breeze behind him he seemed to find pace and control all at once.

With the third ball of his second over, Frank hit the base of Jack Burke's stumps with a glorious yorker. It was a valuable wicket, for Burke is a very difficult chap to remove.

By the way, a remark made by a barracker during Burke's innings the previous day, proves how slow he was at times. He was plodding on, playing the right game, of course, when a loud voice bawled : " Burkie, I wish you were a statue and I was a pigeon ! " What a wonderful remark, made on the spur of the moment in the middle of a Test match. You've got to hand it to these Australian barrackers !

Jack Burke's dismissal, to my mind, was the beginning of the end, and now we were sure that if we could get Neil Harvey out quickly we would win this match.

It was now that Bob Appleyard came into the battle. Richie Benaud was batting, and knowing that he likes to have a go, and hates being kept quiet, Bob was pinning him down on the leg side.

Suddenly Bob tossed one a bit wider outside the leg stump. It seemed to drop more quickly and Richie, mistiming his attempt to hit it for a six, got the top edge. The ball went soaring up towards square leg and as I glanced across to see who was going for it, I felt a cold shiver run down my spine. It was Frank Tyson—not the best of catchers ! The wind had taken the ball, it was spinning as it fell, and Frank hadn't a hope of catching it ! He was nowhere near it.

Suddenly, with the ball only a few inches from the ground, he seemed to make a last-minute grab, his arms outstretched. His feet were wide apart, and he nearly fell over—but the ball was safely in his hands. Frank came up smiling, if a little pale, but Richie was out—a vital wicket.

That was not the only heart-racking moment in that innings, however. There was another—and this time I was concerned. Brian Statham was bowling into the wind, bowling magnificently to left-hander Alan Davidson. Alan snicked the ball very hard, and I had to make a split-second decision whether to go for it or to leave it to Bill Edrich at first slip. Well, I dived for it, flat out, and just got my left hand to it. The pace of the ball swung me round, and as I rolled over with the ball in my left

hand, it dropped out.   Fortunately, as I hit the ground,
I caught it with my right—and it stuck !

I asked Bill afterwards whether the ball would have
carried to first slip.

" I doubt it," he answered.   " You were absolutely
right to go for it."

It is always difficult for a wicket-keeper to decide
whether he should go for a ball or leave it to his slips, but
in this case everything turned out right.   I was glad it
did, for that catch, if missed, might have meant all the
difference between defeat and victory.   However, it
stuck, and I still said :   " We shall be there at the finish,
boys."

Meanwhile, Neil Harvey was still there, and batting
like a master.   His innings of 92 not out was the best
innings I have ever seen him play.   He was completely
on top of the bowling, and that doesn't always happen
with Neil.   I have stood behind him many times, but
however well he has been playing, he has always given
me the impression that he might give a chance.   Yet on
this occasion he never offered even the semblance of a
chance.   He batted really beautifully.   We were sorry
in a way that he did not get a century, but, of course, if
he had done so, it would have cut our slender margin
even more.   It looked at one time as though he and Bill
Johnston would rob us of victory.   Together they had
put on 39 for the last wicket when Frank Tyson enticed
Bill to snick a ball on the leg side.   It was another catch
for me—and we had won a most memorable match.

Thus we were all-square in the series, instead of two
down as looked possible at one stage of the game.

I feel that our victory at Sydney vindicated our pace-
attack policy, for Brian, Frank and Trevor took nineteen
of the twenty Australian wickets, supported, of course,
by some really fine fielding.   How different from the
failures of the first Test. . . .

Before I move on to the next Test, I ought to make
mention of our " twelfth man " who helped us to victory
—at least, we like to believe that his presence brought us

good fortune. I refer to an American friend of ours, Henry Sayen. You may have heard of him. He has flown from Philadelphia on a number of occasions when England have been in a tight spot, and on each occasion he has brought us luck. The first time, I remember, was for the second Test at Lord's in 1953. It looked as though we were heading straight to defeat, but then, on that never-to-be-forgotten day, Trevor Bailey and Willie Watson put up that magnificent stand and saved the day. In the end we won the series.

Then when we were two–one down in the West Indies, Henry Sayen flew out to Jamaica for the last Test and saw us draw level. And now after hearing that we had lost the first Test against Australia, he had flown to Sydney especially to see the second Test. When the match looked as though it was going against us he arrived and he saw us win.

Henry was as delighted as we were and to celebrate he took us all to Prince's and gave us a very good time. He really was a grand friend to all of us.

I only wish Americans played cricket, because I feel they would be very good cricketers. It would also give us a chance to tour their wonderful country.

Although Henry had played on one occasion for the Gentlemen of England, at Lord's, the only American to do so, he did not fully understand the technicalities of our game, because, as he said, it was so different from baseball. I remember him asking me on one occasion : " Now why can't we bribe those two white-coated gentlemen ? How much do you think they will want to give the decisions in our favour ? "

You may laugh, but that was typical of Henry Sayen. He was so enthusiastic that his only thoughts were on helping us to win. We were glad to be able to show him that we *could* win—without bribing the umpires !

From Sydney we went up to Newcastle for one little country match before the Melbourne Test. The Northern Districts usually put out a pretty strong side and we have had many grand tussles there. This time Len

9

thought it advisable for me to play and try to get some batting practice, which I badly needed, for my batting had not been too good up to that time. I was glad I went up to Newcastle—for I found my old batting form.

Before the game I talked to Denis Compton about my batting, and he gave me this advice : " Why don't you go in there and throw caution to the wind ? "

Peter May said much the same. " Give it a bit of hammer, Godfrey," was his advice.

At the start of my innings I was all at sea, but eventually I did hit one, straight over extra cover's head. It did not go for six but very nearly, and it restored my confidence. From that moment I really felt that I could go in, and get among the runs once more. When we went to the third Test in Melbourne I could hardly wait for my turn to bat—and that hadn't happened since we left England. So I am grateful to the skipper for sending me to Newcastle.

Melbourne has always been a favourite ground for England, but the question we selectors had to decide was whether we should change a winning side ? And what about Alec Bedser ? Wasn't Melbourne one of his favourite grounds ? After deliberation, however, we decided to choose the same team as before, except that Denis Compton, now fit again, came in for Tom Graveney. With Australia having Miller back in the side, and Ian Johnson returning as captain instead of Arthur Morris, everything was set for another exciting tussle.

Something happened *before* the match that had a very great bearing on the eventual result—at least, *I* think it did, for I was one of the central characters in this behind the scenes story.

It was obvious to most of us that Len Hutton was beginning to feel the strain of the tour. His back was painful, too, and he intimated to his fellow-selectors that he did not feel fit enough to play, yet he did not want to let the side down.

This caused us considerable concern and when Bill Edrich and I accompanied Len to the Melbourne ground

Canberra, 1955—the members of the M.C.C. team and the Prime Minister's XI, which shows the fine and friendly spirit in which the match was played. Mr. Bob Menzies is seated in the centre of the front row between the two captains, Len Hutton and Lindsay Hassett.

The shot with which Evans won the Ashes in Australia.

early on the first morning of the Test, we decided to try
to persuade him to play. We told him he must play at
all costs. We pointed out the inspiring psychological
effect it would have on the Australians if he were to drop
out now—and, of course, the reverse effect it would have
on our team.

" It doesn't matter if you are a sick man, Len," I told
him. " It doesn't matter if you can hardly stand, you
must skipper us today. Bat first if we win the toss, and
I'm certain we can win this match. We have got them
where we want them, but if you cry off, Len, there's no
knowing what will happen."

It was not easy for Bill and me to talk to our skipper in
that way, but we were sure that Len would appreciate our
concern—and we knew Len ! As you all know, he
agreed to play, and we won the third Test, but I am quite
convinced that had the skipper cried off at the last
minute, the result might easily have been reversed.

The match followed almost exactly the same course as
the Sydney Test, with Australia needing 240 to win in
the last knock.

They lost the Sydney game because of Frank Tyson's
bowling. They lost this one—again because of Frank.
My word, I have seldom seen faster bowling, and he
finished with 7 for 27.

When play opened on the fifth day, Australia were 75
for 2. The match hung in the balance, but we knew if
we could capture Neil Harvey's wicket and get an early
break-through, we would be well on the way to victory.

The first over started, and Frank bowled one down the
leg side. Neil tickled it round the corner, and ran two.
Next ball was a straight one, and Neil played it straight
back. Third ball was again down the leg side. Neil
flicked it round the corner and for some unaccountable
reason—instinct, I suppose—I anticipated the movement.
I leapt across, dived full length and clutched the ball.
Neil was out, caught on the leg side. It was a grand
start. Our tails were up. We were right on top now
and we stayed on top to the end.

I feel that the dismissal of Neil Harvey was the most valuable catch I have ever made, from the point of psychological effect. We all wanted Neil Harvey out, for while he was there Australia always had a chance. So that catch came just at the right moment to inspire us all to drive home the advantage we had gained. It was not the best catch I have ever made, far from it. In actual fact my catch that dismissed Bill Johnston to finish off that Test was a better one. So was my dismissal of Alan Davidson off Brian Statham in Sydney, but from the point of view of value to the side I am sure it was the greatest catch I ever made for England.

However, in case you think I am claiming too much of the credit for our summary dismissal of Australia in that second Melbourne innings, let me pay a big tribute to the whole side. How it had improved. The boys were right on top in the field, and the throwing-in was just what every wicket-keeper dreams about. We were a totally different side from the team that lost in Brisbane. The spirit was wonderful and every one of us was convinced right from the first ball that " We shall be there at the finish." It was that spirit that kept us on top.

The " gates " at Melbourne were absolutely fantastic. For the whole five days the ground was packed tight. Over 300,000 was the total attendance. Unfortunately, since our previous tour, one of the stands had been taken down, and a new double-decker was being erected, but even then a tremendous amount of money was taken— nearly £A48,000—which was certainly good from our point of view, for we knew now that the tour was going to be a financial success.

It was interesting to see how changed Melbourne looked compared with previous tours. Even then the ground was being prepared for the 1956 Olympic Games. One of the big stands had been completely demolished and we were told that it was to be replaced by a huge double-decker that would raise the seating accommodation of the ground to something like 120,000. Melbourne has always been the world's greatest cricket ground, and it will be even greater when another Test series is played there.

The Melbourne ground record of something like 81,000 was set up way back in 1936, but since then the daily attendance has been restricted to around 70,000, for the sake of comfort. Cricket, you know, is not like football, which lasts for less than two hours, and spectators do not mind standing in cramped conditions. When you go to cricket for a whole day, you want to walk around and stretch your legs at times, have a cup of tea and a wash and brush up. That is impossible if all the gangways are blocked, which would be the case if the ground was filled to its utmost capacity, and that is why the Melbourne authorities limit cricket attendances to about 70,000.

With the new stand, however, I see no reason why future Test cricketers should not play before crowds of 120,000, especially if future England teams prove the attraction we were during that 1954–55 tour. Imagine the crowds that will pack Melbourne for a final Test if the two countries are level pegging in the series at two-each! I wonder if I shall have that wonderful experience?

To return to our original subject—with the inspiring knowledge that the tour was an assured financial success, our thoughts turned to the fourth Test, at Adelaide. Leading two–one with two to play, we naturally wanted to win to clinch the rubber. Of course, from the financial point of view, victory for Australia would have meant a decider at Sydney and, perhaps, record-breaking attendances, but we were cricketers and not business-men, and our only thought was to win at Adelaide. The final Test could take care of itself.

What a wonderful psychological effect victory has on a team. In my previous tours it was we who had to do the worrying—worrying about how we could counter the great advantage held by our opponents. Now the boot was on the other foot with a vengeance. It was the Australians who had the worries, and things happened.

Arthur Morris was dropped from the original selection and then reinstated when Ray Lindwall was unable to play. It seemed rather odd to us that a batsman should be recalled for a bowler, especially a bowler of Lindwall's capabilities and experience. The Australians were very certainly in a dilemma. The selectors even called on Ian Johnson to continue as captain, although he was not fit.

One doesn't crow about the opposition's difficulties, but it was such a changed state of affairs in view of our previous experiences in Australia.

Well, we lost the toss at Adelaide, but such was our confidence that we did not mind, although the wicket was a beauty. We knew we had the bowlers to see us through. Yet it was Len's handling of the attack that really won us the match, and the series. Australian batsmen have never liked being pegged down, but on this occasion he was determined to peg them down. The basis of our attack was the pace of Statham and Tyson, helped by Bailey, with Appleyard and Wardle to block up the score.

This then was our plan. We had to keep the runs down to a minimum of 180 for the day if we could possibly do it. As events proved we did better than that—Australia scored only 160, and in the process they lost 4 wickets. It was a great achievement by our bowlers, and if it had not been for Len Maddocks and Ian Johnson adding 92 for the eighth wicket next day, I think we would have had them out for a much smaller score than the 323 which they eventually reached.

In reply, we put up our best Test score so far. Len Hutton was right back in form again, but Alan Davidson's catch that dismissed him was quite fantastic. Bill Johnston bowled him a long hop and Len went back and gave it a mighty clout. We expected Alan Davidson, fielding very close in at short leg, to duck, but he just stood his ground and cupped his hands in front of his tummy—or rather just below—and Len's crisp pull went straight into Alan Davidson's hands. How he saw it I don't

know, because the sun was right in his eyes, but the ball
nestled there. A great catch! Len was disappointed.
He needed only twenty runs for his 100. However, he
gave us a good start, and at close of play we were 230 for
3 with Denis and Colin Cowdrey still there.

Unfortunately, for us, Australia did not call for the
new ball before close of play, but took it first thing in the
morning. Actually, it was a good move by Ian Johnson,
because in the first overs next morning Denis and Colin
were out for the addition of only two runs. Almost
before the game had started, Trevor and I were out there
facing this new ball. As I have told you, my batting
had not been good during the tour, but after that merry
innings at Newcastle when I got 60-odd, I felt like hitting
the ball all over Adelaide—which, in fact, is exactly what
happened.

Perhaps I was a bit lucky. I was dropped once, although it was a difficult chance. Keith Miller bowled
me a snorter just outside the off stump. I tried to play
it down, but it caught the edge, and Burke, at fourth slip,
grabbed it—but couldn't hold it. Apart from that
chance, however, I felt absolutely confident, and I was
soon having a go. Then when Trevor and I had put
on 51 I was caught " behind " off Richie Benaud. I
was very disappointed at getting out for only 37 ; however, we were now very much nearer the Australian
score.

I had only just reached the dressing-room when a
terrific roar went up. I was certain it was another wicket,
but a moment later somebody rushed in to tell me that
Johnny Wardle had hit a terrific six right out of the
ground.

Eventually we managed to gain a slender lead on the
first innings, and we thought we were in for another tense
fight, but something happened to the Australians. They
seemed quite demoralised and completely collapsed,
leaving us only 94 to win.

I think we could be excused for imagining that we were
on an easy thing, but Keith Miller had vastly different

ideas. Opening the bowling he took our first 3 wickets and the score was only 18.

Keith was going flat out and fairly hurling the ball down the wicket. Len, Bill and Colin were back in the dressing-room, and the tension mounted rapidly.

Nobody spoke, although facial expressions told their own tales. Some of the boys stood silently on the balcony watching the game, others walked about outside. I sat inside reading a book, not only to keep my mind off the game but because with three wickets down I knew I might soon have to pad up. I had not long to wait. There came a deafening roar from the crowd. Peter May was out, and the matter of his dismissal was a topic of discussion for some time afterwards.

Peter was not given out—he walked out ! He hit the ball hard and low to extra cover, where Keith Miller dived and caught the ball, or appeared to do so. Actually, in rolling over, Keith let the ball drop to the floor, but Peter did not see this—he was already on his way back to the pavilion. In disgust, Keith threw the ball back to the bowler, but nobody said a word and Peter was allowed to leave the wicket. Denis, at the other end, seeing all that had happened, tried to call Peter back, but owing to the thunderous din of the excited crowd, he went unheard. In any case Peter thought he was out.

It was rather difficult to know what really happened, but after the match Keith explained that he thought he held the ball long enough to claim the catch, although I am sure he was wrong. I have always understood that if a fielder rolls over on the ground as he clutches the ball, that is part of the catch, so if the ball pops out and touches the ground, the catch is not complete. If that is correct, then Peter was not out. However in this particular instance it made no difference to the result.

Denis and Trevor continued to battle along and the score gradually crept up. Then, with only four more needed, Trevor was out. I was next man in, and my only thought was to finish it off as quickly as possible—all or nothing, for I knew we still had a few wickets to go.

When I reached the wicket to join Denis, there was one ball to come. I slashed at it, missed it and it went for one bye. That single took me to the other end, where Keith Miller was still on. Off his second ball I pushed him down to third man, and we ran a quick two, although Denis, at the other end, did not want to run the second. I imagined he thought I was taking too many risks. . . . Anyway, two it was, and I faced Keith again. His next ball was a real snorter. I let it go—I could do little else !

The next ball he pitched right up on to the stumps, and I had an almighty swing at it. It went for four. We were there !

In the dressing-room afterwards, Denis told me why he was reluctant to run two off that shot of mine. He had been offered £5 if he hit the winning run, but only on condition that he told *no one* !

Well, I was sorry that Denis lost that fiver, but how was I to know ? In any case, it mattered little who hit the winning run—so long as we won !

The final Test, at Sydney, came as something of an anti-climax, for rain spoiled it. The first three days were completely blank owing to the weather. In fact, it was not until after lunch on the fourth day that play was possible.

England, batting first on a wicket that had been covered throughout the incessant rains, totalled 371 for 7 wickets declared, thanks to a very fine 111 from Tom Graveney. He was in his greatest run-getting form, for he was at the wicket for only 150 minutes, and completed his hundred with four fours off Keith Miller.

Australia replied with 222 and then, following-on, were 118 for 6 when the match ended. It was one of the worst batting displays I had ever seen by an Australian Test side, and I am quite sure that even if the weather had not ruined the game as a contest, we should have won.

Apart from some grand bowling by Johnny Wardle, the only other incident of note in the match was the performance of Ray Lindwall, who captured his 100th wicket in Tests against England and became the first fast bowler to reach such a landmark in the whole history of Test cricket.

I shall always remember it because mine was one of the wickets which gave Ray his wonderful record. That was his 99th, and Trevor Bailey provided him with the 100th.

There was considerable criticism of our action. Many people said that we were wrong to throw our wickets away just to give Ray his record, but there was no disagreement among the players. When I went out to join Trevor at the wicket, Ray had 98 wickets to his credit, and it looked very much as though this would be the last Test appearance of this great-hearted cricketer. So when we heard that Len Hutton was anxious to declare in an effort to win the match, Trevor and I decided to " have a go ", even though it might mean losing our wickets.

Ray put five men on the boundary, and I quickly skied one to mid-wicket. Then Trevor tried to sweep one of Ray's fastest balls to leg, a shot which he had no possible hope of making successfully, and was bowled.

Did our action belittle Ray's performance of taking 100 wickets against England ? I do not think so. Personally, I felt delighted that I was able to help him to reach such a memorable landmark. Remember, there was no question of England losing the Test. In fact, we still had a chance to win, as was proved when we nearly pulled it off. Had Trevor and I tried to stay, even that chance might have been lost. So the criticisms that we had let down our country were entirely without foundation.

Tests between England and Australia have always been fought out under such a fight-to-the-finish tension, that it surely is grand to feel that there is still some sentiment left in the game. In any case, is there anyone in cricket who would begrudge Ray Lindwall the achievement of a record that must have been his dream over the years ?

We were all gratified after the match to read in the Australian papers a report by Keith Miller, Test star and journalist by profession, that " the action of Evans and Trevor Bailey giving their wickets to Ray Lindwall was a gesture that honoured a great fast bowler. . . ."

CHAPTER IX

The Rubber Against Jack Cheetham's Men— 1955

HAVING COME STRAIGHT FROM RETAINING THE ASHES in Australia, we were now undisputedly the leading cricket country in the world and looking forward to meeting the South Africans, who had brought over a young side, in the hope of putting up a good show. Eight of the tourists had been to England before, and although some of them were quite young at the time of their first visit, the experience gained on that tour was expected to be invaluable to them and to their side this time.

England naturally selected as many as possible of the successful side that had toured " Down Under " for the opening Test at Nottingham. The only exceptions were Don Kenyon, the Worcestershire opening batsman, who was selected because Len Hutton was suffering from a recurrence of his unfortunate back trouble, and Ken Barrington, the young Surrey batting star, who was making his Test debut. In Len's absence, Peter May was asked to captain the side, and he did a right good captain's job in winning the toss.

To-date, the South Africans had not really shown to advantage. The weather during the early part of the tour was extremely cold, and cricketers are never at their best under wintry conditions, especially if they come straight from warm sunshine. In warm climates, such as South Africa, players have no need to wear sweaters, and, therefore, movements and reactions must be quicker than when they are forced to wear one—or even two, as is necessary sometimes in this country. This may have had much to do with the South Africans' early form.

Anyway, to return to the Nottingham Test. Don Kenyon had been rather a failure in his previous Test appearances, but his mammoth scores in County matches with Worcestershire early in the season marked him as the obvious choice to take over from Len Hutton, and now that Tom Graveney had established himself so well as Len's opening partner on the latter part of the Australian tour, he and Don faced the fast bowling of Neil Adcock, from Transvaal, and the left-hand medium pace of tall Trevor Goddard.

Fortune follows the brave, and Don Kenyon was fortunate in his brave innings when he was dropped at forward short leg by Hughie Tayfield before he had reached double figures. But Don weathered the storm well and he and Tom put on 91 before being parted.

It was still cold, and on the field it was obvious that the South Africans could not give of their best, even though they were trying so hard. Jack Cheetham had no outstanding stars, like Dudley Nourse, Alan Melville, and Bruce Mitchell, but as a side they relied entirely on their team spirit and high degree of fitness. This had brought them a great reputation in the field. Unfortunately, the weather was entirely against them for brilliant fielding at Nottingham, and, in consequence, they fell below the standard we were expecting. But there was no doubt later on that they were a brilliant fielding side, worthily proving the old saying that catches win matches, but not with cold hands at Nottingham.

England finished with a score of 334, a very useful total in present-day cricket, but by now the crowds at Trent Bridge were eagerly waiting to see Frank Tyson and Brian Statham open the England attack. In fact, they cheered like mad when our last wicket fell, but then, as in most Tests, just as Tyson began his first run-up, a tense silence fell over the ground. I recall that silence at Nottingham so distinctly. It persisted as Frank charged up to bowl his first ball to left-hander Goddard, and then a tremendous gasp broke out all over the ground. That first ball was just short of a good length, and just outside the leg stump.   Goddard had to move very quickly out of the way or the ball would have hit him, because he certainly hadn't time to play any shot at it.   The Nottingham crowd were back in their element. It must have brought many of them memories of " Lol " Larwood and Bill Voce.

It was Brian Statham, however, who struck the first blow for us, getting Trevor Goddard l.b.w.   Goddard is a difficult player to dislodge.   He has a small back lift for a left-hander, and watches the ball very closely, so his wicket was indeed a good start to the series for us.

It was not long before we were into the middle of the batting order.   Brian helped in the dismissal of John Waite for nought.   John and Jackie McGlew tried to take two as Brian picked up on the boundary edge, but Brian has a wonderful throw, and the ball came straight and true to me right over the stumps, and John was a yard out of his ground.   It was a magnificent throw.

Then Frank Tyson's turn came for wickets.   He got Russell Endean l.b.w., and immediately followed by knocking Roy McLean's stumps for " a Burton ".   This was a sad blow for South Africa.   With only McGlew and Jack Cheetham making any reasonable score, and with Bob Appleyard and Johnny Wardle finishing off the tail, we made them follow-on 153 runs behind.

For some time after the start of their second innings, it seemed that we had made a mistake.   McGlew and Goddard never looked like getting out, and the first wicket did not fall until they had put 73 on the board. But then Frank really did get going.   He finished off the innings with the wonderful analysis of 6 for 28 in 21 overs, so it is no exaggeration to say that South Africa were humbled by the pace of Frank Tyson.   It was certainly his match.

What I liked about the South African batting was that although they were beaten by sheer pace, they showed no lack of courage.   They got behind the ball all the time, a totally different approach from the Australians, who give themselves more room to play their shots off

Above: England's wicket-keeper shows the little finger which he broke in the 1955 Test at Manchester to Miss Pat Smythe (*left*), Britain's champion lady show-jumper, and Miss Diane Leather, record-breaking athlete. They met at the Dorchester Hotel during rehearsals for the Lord's Taverners' Ball.

Right: Godfrey Evans takes a leg-side catch off Frank Tyson to dismiss Neil Harvey in the third Test, at Melbourne. The author considers this the most valuable catch he has ever taken for his side. Colin Cowdrey leaps for joy in the leg-slip position.

The England team at Nottingham, 1955, where Peter May captained the Test XI for the first time. Left to right: (back row) Barrington, Appleyard, Tyson, Graveney, Statham, Kenyon; (front row) Evans,

this type of bowling.   The batting of the South Africans
was inclined to be on the slow side, but in Roy McLean
they possessed the best stroke-maker in cricket today,
and I felt that given warmer weather, and better form,
they would prove a difficult side to beat.

With a victory to our credit at Nottingham—by an
innings and 5 runs—we looked forward to the next encounter at Lord's.

To play in a Test match at Lord's is the ambition of
every cricketer, and I know that all the South Africans
were hoping and praying that they would fulfil that
ambition.   By now the weather was warming up, and
the tourists were beginning to blend into a team.   England were without Appleyard and Tyson, so it looked on
paper as though South Africa had a better chance than
at Nottingham.

Peter May won the toss again and elected to bat.
From the first few overs from Neil Adcock and Peter
Heine, it was obvious to all of us that it was a very fast
and lively wicket.   I hesitate to think what would have
happened had we lost the toss and South Africa had
batted against Tyson !

Peter Heine, one of the Africaans in the side, had had
little experience of international cricket, but he had
made such strides since his arrival in the country, that
the South African selectors had no hesitation in choosing
him.   His selection meant that the tourists had a very
good attack to open with in Adcock and Heine, with
Goddard to block up the scoring, Peter Mansell for leg-
spin, and Hughie Tayfield with his off-spin, to complete
a well-balanced attack.

In those first few overs, several of the balls just short
of a length whipped up chest high to the batsmen, who
had quite a struggle to get runs.   Added to this, the
South African fielding was superb. Jackie McGlew,
covering the off-side anywhere from cover to mid-off,
frequently dived full length to cut off what appeared to
be certain fours, leaving the batsmen with only singles
—and sometimes without a run at all.

Peter Heine, who did most of the bowling and the wicket-taking, made a great start to his Test career, and judging from his form in that match at Lord's, he can be assured of a great future in South African cricket. His 5 for 60 was one of the factors that forced England's dismissal for the poor score of 133.

This was not very good, but we were still interested to see how South Africa would fare on this lively wicket, because although we were without Tyson, we had Brian Statham and Freddie Trueman, who, while not quite so quick as Frank, is a very fine fast bowler. Fred Titmus, the young Middlesex all-rounder, was also given his debut.

The South African innings started with shocks for me. The first ball I received and the first from Brian brought a wicket. McGlew got a faint edge, and it was " caught Evans bowled Statham . . . o ". A second wicket quickly followed. Freddie Trueman opened the bowling from the Nursery End and in his first over Goddard was out—and I had taken another catch. I remember the ball swinging down to Goddard, and, being a left-hander, it was an in-swinger, which he tried to turn round the corner. I saw the ball leave the bat and dived full length to my right, to hold it about a foot off the ground. I was never more thankful to catch a ball, because with our score at 133, we could not afford to miss any chances.

Well, 7 for 2 was a good start—and then we had a few set-backs. Jack Cheetham went fairly quickly, but then Russell Endean and Roy McLean got together and started tousing our bowling. Roy finished with 142— having been given six lives into the bargain. It is to his credit, however, that these lives made no difference to his tactics, and he continued to play the glorious shots that only a stroke-maker of his class can.

When Roy was here on the previous tour, I recall Denis Compton saying to me : " This young boy Roy McLean is one of the best stroke-makers I have ever seen." Those words were beginning to ring true.

Anyhow, we continued to attack as best we could, and

The author "goes to ground" in catching Goddard (South Africa) on the leg side off Freddie Trueman, at Lord's. This is regarded as one of the author's most spectacular catches. It appears that Fred Titmus agrees.

John Waite, the South African wicket-keeper, sends the middle stump flying in an unsuccessful attempt to run out the author at Nottingham in the first Test of 1955.

Three Kent wicket-keepers—Godfrey Evans (*left*), Jack Hubble (*centre*), and Leslie Ames—enjoying a toast at Canterbury.

Lord Cornwallis, High Sheriff of Kent, presents Colin Cowdrey (*left*) and the author with silver cigarette-boxes on behalf of the Kent C.C., the Kent Association of Cricket Clubs, the Kentish Men and the Men of Kent, and the Kent Playing Fields Association, in appreciation of their performances during the successful Australian tour of 1954–55.

once Roy was out of the way, it was only left-hander Headley Keith who caused us any trouble. Eventually I stumped Peter Heine off Johnny Wardle and their score of 304 was complete—a match-winning total, we thought, and we knew we had to make a lot of runs in the second innings to have any chance of winning this second Test.

Don Kenyon was out in Goddard's first over—another low score for Don—and then we saw Peter May and Tom Graveney at their best. They put on 132 before being parted. Then Denis Compton showed us that bad knee or no bad knee, he was still one of the finest batsmen in the game.

Hughie Tayfield bowled splendidly and finished with five of our wickets. Everybody who sees Hughie bowling thinks that he should be collared as it were, but believe me, Hughie is full of guile, and a far better bowler than he looks. When I was batting I thought I was hitting one past him on the ground, but I was not quite to the pitch of it, and he took a very hard return catch.

353 was our final score, leaving South Africa to get 182 for victory. They might have got them, too—who knows?—but Jack Cheetham was hit on the elbow off a rising ball from Freddie Trueman, and had to retire. I was surprised afterwards at the number of people I met who thought that it was done intentionally by Freddie. I can assure any of you who feel the same, that this was not the case.

What really happened, as I saw it from my position behind the stumps, was this. Freddie bowled a bouncer to Jack, and Jack, instead of moving out of the way and letting it pass, allowed the ball to hit him. It was sheer misfortune that the ball hit him on the point of the elbow, which, at the best of times, is very painful, and this fast delivery almost paralysed his arm. There was never any ill-feeling over the matter, because Jack openly said it was his own fault, and I really think it was his own fault, too.

Anyway, Brian Statham was right on top of his form.

10

Bowling unchanged throughout the innings, with that penetrative accuracy that makes him such a great attacker, he took 7 for 39 in 29 overs. That's accuracy for you if you like ! We gave Brian a great hand—and so did the crowd—and, I may say, so did the South Africans !

So here we were, two up and three to go. If we won at Manchester in the third Test, it would be a most disappointing tour for the South Africans. So they really had to make an outstanding effort at Old Trafford to keep the interest alive and to ensure the turnstiles clicking for the sake of the English Counties and the South African Board of Control, who rely so much on these tours to keep them financially straight.

Changes were necessary in our side once more. Frank Tyson was now fit again, but his partner, Brian Statham, was unable to play owing to a strained muscle. But who better to take Brian's place than the " Old Firm " of Alec Bedser ? Colin Cowdrey, the success of the tour " Down Under ", was also brought in for his first Test in England, and Tony Lock replaced Johnny Wardle as the left-arm spinner.

Peter May won the toss for the third time running, and Kenyon and Graveney once more opened. Alas, once again our opening pair failed. (It is a long time since the days of Len Hutton and Cyril Washbrook, when we were fairly certain of a good start to our innings.) The scoreboard read " 1 for 2 ", and then " 2 for 22 " —yes, we were at it again ! However, we were fortunate in having Denis at his best, and he, with the help of Peter May and, later, Trevor Bailey, made a magnificent 158. I think Denis must like Old Trafford ! Anyway, he gave the scoreboard respectability and we finished with a total of 284.

The weather at Manchester certainly played havoc with the forecasts, as throughout this magnificent Test we enjoyed some of the best cricket weather one could possibly expect in this country. This had some bearing, I'm sure, on the performance of the South Africans.

Their fielding had now reached the height of brilliance that we had expected when they first arrived here. Their bowling, too, was much improved. If only they could get three or four of their batsmen in form at the same time, then, by jove, we knew we should have to work hard for victory.

This is exactly what happened. Jackie McGlew, John Waite and Paul Winslow all scored hundreds, and when they finally declared at 521 for 8, things looked very black for England.

Alec Bedser, who had lost some of his fire, was not the effective partner for Tyson that Statham would have been. It is interesting to recall that Larwood and Voce were much better as a combination than Larwood and Tate, and now Tyson and Statham had become our finest attacking combination. Alec and Frank did not seem to blend into an effective partnership.

With regard to Paul Winslow's innings, it was quite obvious that he has no fear of " the nervous nineties ". He completed his " ton " with a six, one of three in his innings. One of these was certainly the biggest hit I have ever seen—right over the Stretford end into the park at the back of the stand.

It was during the opening spell on the Saturday morning that Frank Tyson bowled an in-swinger to left-hander Goddard. It was a little wide of the mark, and went curling away down the leg side. I moved over quickly to take what I thought a normal delivery, but as it passed the wicket it started to swing or drift away from me. I thought for a moment that it was going for four byes, so I had to make a last minute lunge to cut the ball off. In doing so I twisted my hand and the ball actually struck the back part of my little finger. I stopped the ball all right, but a violent pain shot through my hand, and I turned to Tom Graveney and said : " By jove, that hurts ! "

A wicket-keeper gets many of these blows, and the pain usually lasts for only two or three balls, or possibly an over, and then goes. But this time the pain did not go, and when we eventually got the wicket of Keith, I took my glove off to look at my little finger. I realised then that this was no ordinary knock. Something really serious was wrong. It was bent, swollen and jet black in colour, but when you are playing in a Test, there is only one thing to do—carry on.

I explained to Peter May, our skipper, that I had hurt my finger and he asked me if I would like somebody else to keep wicket. Without hesitation I replied :

" No—not unless it's absolutely necessary. It's so unfair to the person who takes over the gloves."

As I learned later, when my finger was X-rayed, it was broken in two places, and continuing to keep wicket all day had literally knocked all the marrow out of the joints. The finger was put in plaster, and I knew I would be unable to keep wicket again in this Test at least.

We were now well adrift so far as runs were concerned, and we knew we should need plenty in the second innings if we were to make any sort of reply. Fortunately, Peter and Denis were again in great form, although it was Peter's turn for a hundred this time, while Colin Cowdrey made amends for his single in the first innings by hitting " half a ton ".

During this time, the South Africans were working out how much time they would have to win the match—for they were determined to win this time, knowing that we had lost 6 wickets for 274. Trevor Bailey was still there, and he stuck to his task well. But when we lost Titmus, Tyson and then Alec Bedser, I decided to go out to see what I could do. I had already had a " net " to see whether I could hold the bat or not, and had cut the little finger off my batting glove. As a matter of fact, I was surprised at the ease with which I could hold the bat, for the plaster made my little finger stick out away from the handle of the bat.

If there had been no chance of our winning or avoiding defeat, there would have been no point in me going out to face the music. As it was, if I could make enough runs, or even stay there long enough for someone else to

get them, we could not only save ourselves from defeat,
but there was still an outside chance of victory. I had
the option of batting or remaining off the field, although
Peter May told me he thought it might be better if I did
not bat.

" Of course I'll bat," was my answer. " And what's
more, I'll make some runs as well."

That was no idle boast. I really did feel like batting,
and making runs, too. I found to my surprise—unaccountable, I fear—that I could see the ball clearly
right from the start, and once out in the middle I almost
forgot my broken finger. Every " four " I hit to the
fence I realised was giving England an extra chance.
Every over I stayed would make South Africa's task
more difficult. So in that mood, I took the bull by the
horns and hit out at every ball off which I thought I
could get runs. And it worked. (Some people say I
should always bat with a broken finger !)

Eventually, when I was caught by Roy McLean in the
deep off Hughie Tayfield, Trevor and I had put on
48 runs for the last wicket, my share being 36. This
left us a fighting chance, and was a challenge to South
Africa that we knew they would be bound to accept.

They DID accept it, and straightway started to attack.
I am afraid I was sitting in the dressing-room watching
and wishing I was out there. Tom Graveney had taken
over my job behind the stumps, and this gave the South
Africans a chance for some snappy runs. They even
took singles when the ball passed the wicket off Frank
Tyson's bowling. That was not Tom's fault entirely, for
it is difficult to stop batsmen taking those quick singles,
but with an experienced wicket-keeper, there is more
chance of running out one of a pair who are audacious
enough to take such risks.

I must be fair to Tom and say that although he was
doing a job to which he was not in any way accustomed
or experienced, he did it really well. It meant, however, that in keeping to the bowling of Alec Bedser, for
instance, he had to stand back. Thus, the South African

batsmen were able to take advantage of this, by standing out of their ground to Alec, and, therefore, had more chance of scoring runs off him.

It was during the last over of the match that John Waite drove Tyson through the covers for four runs, to win a wonderfully exciting game. Remember, they had only three wickets left, so you can tell how thrilling a finish it was.

This win put South Africa in a better frame of mind, and although I was unable to play in the next two Tests at Leeds and the Oval, their well-merited win at Headingley squared the series at two-all, and revived interest throughout the whole country.

England eventually won the series with a victory at the Oval. I had the pleasure of sitting in the South African dressing-room to watch part of that Test.

Jack Cheetham and his men returned home with many happy memories of the tour. They left many friends behind them, for their fighting qualities after being two-down after two games, will be talked about for many years to come. They certainly showed us how to field, and I am sure they taught many County sides that fielding is a far more important factor than many cricketers seem to realise.

Well done, South Africa ! It was grand to have you with us again !

CHAPTER X

Cricket with the New Zealanders

I HAVE NOW VISITED NEW ZEALAND ON THREE OCCASIONS, and have also played against them in one Test series in this country. These have been among my most enjoyable experiences, for the New Zealanders are grand chaps, yet there is no doubt at all that they do not reach the high standard attained by the other cricketing countries.

Why is this? Well, looking into the reasons I feel that the lack of playing facilities in New Zealand is a great handicap to them. Although the climate out there closely resembles our own, New Zealand is a hilly country, divided into two islands, which brings certain travel difficulties. Then again, cricket out there is organised rather on the same basis as our own English club cricket, with only Saturday afternoon games and very few representative matches.

New Zealand, too, is sparsely populated, which means fewer players, and, of course, fewer clubs. There is no " Grade " cricket as in Australia, so that when a really outstanding player—Bert Sutcliffe, for instance—comes to the fore, he has little chance to better himself, playing, as he does, against the same grade of player each week. In other words, there is not enough variation of opposition to enable a player to make the necessary progress to real class. New Zealand is 1,000 miles from Australia, and 15,000 miles from England, and that in itself is a decided disadvantage.

However, not only is there a lack of opposition, there is also a paucity of clubs—and of players, too. New Zealand is an agricultural country, and as most of the keen young cricketers are on the farms or in industry, they cannot devote much time to the sport, and when that happens, the standard of cricket must fall.

Let us look a little more deeply into this question, for, of course, whatever the standard of cricket, New Zealand do compete in Test matches and overseas tours, despite their limited playing resources. There are faults with their attitude to cricket. For instance, we bowled them out for 26 during the last Test we played against them— and that was on a wicket on which we should not have been surprised had they scored 226.

The batsmen in New Zealand seem afraid to attack the bowling. I am convinced that they would do much better if they played more shots rather than the defensive cricket which is such a feature of post-war New Zealand batting. There is no doubt about their enthusiasm for the game, and of their keen determination to do well against the M.C.C., especially before their own people. This may cause them to try too hard, and, in consequence, they do not make the shots for fear of losing their wickets. This makes for dull cricket, as we all know.

Another reason for this defensive batting attitude is the umpiring. In New Zealand very rarely is an l.b.w. decision given. Ernie Toshack, the Australian, was telling me that in one match in New Zealand he made forty-eight appeals for l.b.w., yet not one was allowed. This reticence of the umpires to acknowledge the leg-before-wicket rule must automatically make the batsman step in front of his wicket, knowing that he will be safe should the ball rap his pad, and, of course, this must curtail his range of strokes—and his playing of shots. The sooner the l.b.w. rule is tackled in the right manner by their umpires, the better it will be for New Zealand cricket. Covering up with the pads is the ruination of any form of bright, attacking batsmanship.

At the moment, New Zealand have no fast bowlers— not as we have come to know fast bowlers during recent years. This must also be a decided disadvantage and puts a brake on progress, so far as international competition is concerned. Not only do New Zealand batsmen get little practice against good fast bowling, but the captain has no pace-men at his command, so they are on a losing wicket whichever way you look at it.

I am not suggesting that New Zealand have no good bowlers, far from it. Their spinners are excellent, but apart from these chaps they seem to rely too much on the ordinary medium pacer—the sort of chap we know as a straight " up-and-downer ". In consequence, New Zealand's cricket has got rather into a rut, and that is not good for their game in general.

Please do not think that I am contemptuous of New Zealand cricket. I am merely trying to fathom the reasons why they are not among the leading cricket countries at the moment. Their recent tour in India and Pakistan and their home Test series with the West Indies, proved, I feel, that there is something lacking in their general outlook on the game.

The team is not without its stars, however. In Bert Sutcliffe they have one of the world's finest left-hand batsmen, and John Reid is an all-rounder worthy to rank among the world's best. But two men do not make a team. I admit that there are three or four more who would make any County side in this country, but I feel the New Zealand authorities would find it difficult to choose a really strong Test ELEVEN at the moment. Remember, it is only courting disaster to place reliance on only two or three men in any Test side.

It is a great pity that New Zealand's cricket is at such a low ebb, for anyone who has been to their delightful country will agree with me that there is nothing wrong with their enthusiasm for the game. I can speak from experience and say that I found this enthusiasm equal to that of the Australians, and I feel sure that if only more players could be found, and more chances given to those players for the acquisition of big-match experience against first-class opposition, then the general enthusiasm for the game would soon be reflected in an all-round improvement in New Zealand cricket.

I do not despair in any way. Cricket is played in the schools out there, and much good work is being done by

English coaches. These men, with the help of the few outstanding home players, will do much, I feel sure, to remedy the lack of enterprise that has so stilted the New Zealanders' approach to the game.

Talking recently about the shortage of players and the lack of spare time that most young New Zealanders can spare for the game, I recall a personal experience that may throw some light on this topic.

When my wife and I were in New Zealand during our last tour, we met Len Bisley and his wife at their home. Talking cricket, Len told me of some of the difficulties that confront them so far as active participation in sport is concerned. Despite the fact that he is a busy company director, he goes three times a week to night school. In his class, he said, were two doctors, a dentist, a lawyer, and two more company directors—all eager to learn about building their own houses, making furniture, and all the hundred and one jobs necessary in the running of a house and home.

I was so interested that I went along with Len to see for myself. I did actually learn something—how to make a dovetailed joint. It cost me nothing, and the tutor was an expert. Len told me that he had helped to build his own house, and had made all manner of alterations and improvements to it, through the knowledge gained at night school. The womenfolk also attend to learn about cooking and dressmaking.

Labour is short, and costly, in New Zealand, and this may be a primary reason why the people out there spend so much time doing their own jobs. In consequence, they have little spare time for sport, and certainly little to devote to cricket, much as they love the game.

In fairness to New Zealand, it must also be pointed out that they lack funds to finance projects that might help to improve their standard of cricket. This is due mainly to the few first-class matches played in New Zealand, for, remember, there are only four leading clubs.

No one could complain of the New Zealander's high

degree of sportsmanship. When we were last there, we played to very large crowds, who were very loyal to the Mother Country. Even when we bowled them out for 26, the crowds went home very happy. They did not mind being beaten by a better side—particularly as that side was the M.C.C. Unlike some of the other countries we visit, the New Zealander takes his cricket quietly in a spirit of real enjoyment, rather than of extreme partisanship.

With one really good fast bowler, a class wicket-keeper, and two or three top-class batsmen to back up Bert Sutcliffe, I am sure that New Zealand could hold their own in the world of Test cricket. One day these men may come along, and when they do, New Zealand will rise to a position among the world's best. May that day soon come!

Even as I write, I hear over the radio that the New Zealanders have achieved their first ever Test victory, against a very formidable West Indies side. Perhaps this is a start on their road to the top in international cricket.

CHAPTER XI

Random Reflections on 'Keeping and 'Keepers

AFTER KEEPING WICKET DURING THOUSANDS OF INNINGS —goodness knows how many!—I suppose I can claim to know something about the job I have studied so closely, both from my own angle and from that of other great stumpers.

Throughout the year I receive many letters from young 'keepers asking for advice, and at cricket gatherings which I attend I am always being asked questions about the job, particularly about my five " wicket-keeping commandments ". I discussed these fairly fully in my previous book, *Behind the Stumps*, but because of the many requests I have received I hope you will forgive me if I repeat them here.

Much has happened since I first drew up these five primary wicket-keeping points, but I still have found no cause to change them. So here they are.

Point No. 1—the 'keeper must have a good view of the ball. When I go to the wicket I take up my stance with my left foot behind the off stump—providing the batsman is a right-hander, of course. I scratch a line straight behind the stump and that is the mark for my left foot. The right foot takes up a normal position corresponding to the left. This position enables me to get a good view of the bowler and the ball.

I have seen some young 'keepers take up a stance with one foot on either side of the wicket, which means that they have to bend the body sideways to see the bowler as he delivers, and this throws the whole body off balance. One cannot move quickly from an off-balanced position, and that is a primary fault, for one of the essentials to good wicket-keeping is quickness of movement from the crouched position.

156

That brings me automatically to Point No. 2—to be evenly balanced on both feet. Remember, the 'keeper has to move quickly to right or left, often with split-second reaction, and if the weight is not evenly balanced on BOTH feet, that is almost impossible. I cannot stress too strongly this question of balance. The wicket-keeper does not know just where the ball is going when it is delivered—even the bowler doesn't know sometimes!— so he must be prepared to move to right OR left in the twinkling of an eye. If he has his body weight on one foot, then he is going to be beaten for speed.

Point No. 3—the 'keeper must watch the ball from the moment the bowler starts his run. In other words, one hundred per cent. concentration on the ball. Wicket-keeping demands complete concentration. There is no chance to relax behind the stumps. If the 'keeper is inclined to take things easy, then he would be better off the field. There is no time to start looking around the field, or adjusting your pads or gloves once the bowler starts his run, unless, of course, you want to miss chances and pile up the " Extras " total.

So settle down into a comfortable position, get a good view of the ball, concentrate from the moment the bowler starts his run, and with plenty of practice you should be confident enough to take those difficult balls on the leg side.

I am often asked how I manage to take so many balls —and so many catches—outside the leg stump. There is only one answer—concentration, and a sense of antici-pation, which, I admit, comes from experience. Yet I am certain that if the young 'keeper sets his mind to it, and follows out those first three basic principles, he should be able to take more balls outside the leg stump than he misses.

Now for Point No. 4—do not snatch at the ball. In other words, when the ball is coming towards you, don't go to meet it. If you do, invariably it will smash against your gloves and bounce out. As the ball meets your gloves, move your hands backwards in the direction in which the ball is travelling—only a fraction, of course, and then when the ball is neatly nestling in your gloves you are all right. So don't snatch, but ride, or give, with the ball.

Point No. 5—whenever practicable try to get your body behind the ball. Your body is your second line of defence. However good a wicket-keeper you are, there will be times when the wicket is a little spiteful, or your judgment may not be absolutely perfect, that you will not be able to gather the ball cleanly in your gloves. In such cases, if your body is behind the ball you will at least be able to prevent it running through for byes, or deflect it for somebody else to field.

I could recall many instances in Test matches when the ball has been outside the leg stump, and in my efforts to get across to it I have missed a clean " take " with my gloves, but because I have had my body in the line of flight, the ball has hit my pads and gone to short-leg. Yet if I had just stretched out my hands to grab, and not moved my body behind my hands, I should have conceded four byes. Well, no one wants to give away unnecessary byes, so get your body behind the ball whenever it is practicable.

I say practicable because there are occasions when this is not the best thing to do. For instance, a batsman is facing a leg-spinner and dashes down the wicket to rather a wide one outside the off stump, and misses the ball. Now, if the wicket-keeper tries to get his body behind the ball, he is so far away from the wicket when the ball arrives, that it is more than likely that he will not be able to reach it.

In that case, the 'keeper must use the sway of the body to reach across to the right to gather the ball and then sway back over the stumps. Normally, however, I would advocate getting the body behind the ball for medium pace and slow bowling if " extras " are to be saved.

There is one other point. The batsman snicks the ball, and you do not make a clean catch, but if the ball hits your body you are given a second chance of a catch.

I remember one particular instance. It was in the 1951 Test at Brisbane, when Freddie Brown was bowling and Sam Loxton was batting. Freddie spun the ball a little and it bounced a bit short. Sam square-cut it, but he did not get it quite in the middle of the bat. The ball hit the top edge, flew off, hit me on the chest and bounced upward. Fortunately, I was right behind the ball, so as it bounced upward and forward off my chest, I managed to fling myself forward and grab it. If I had not had my body behind the ball, it would have been four byes, instead of a catch.

So there are my five " wicket-keeping commandments ". They have been the basis for my own success behind the stumps, although, of course, I must stress the importance of practice. It is all very well to KNOW how to do a job properly, but it is the execution of the job that counts, and I maintain that no cricketer can achieve any sort of success behind the stumps without regular and rigorous practice.

Equipment plays a big part, too. Gloves and pads must be right. They must fit, and they must be comfortable. Most people would agree that the most comfortable clothes are old, or at least, old enough to have taken on some of the wearer's own shape. The same applies to wicket-keeping equipment.

I am fully aware that equipment wears out and must be replaced, but new gloves and pads are too stiff and starchy to make for good wicket-keeping. This " newness ", therefore, must be broken down before they can effectively serve their full purpose. No 'keeper can do his job properly behind the stumps wearing stiff equipment.

Just after I left school and went to play for a local club, the captain said to me : " I hear you have kept wicket once or twice, so would you mind acting as stumper today ? "

I was quite agreeable, and the captain threw me a brand-new pair of gloves. Naturally, the club thought they were the last word in style, and I had to admit, when I looked at them, that they were a very good pair, although I would have preferred older equipment. Then the skipper handed me a brand-new pair of pads straight out of the paper in which they were wrapped by the dealer.

I did not want to appear ungrateful, so I proceeded to strap on those pads and don the gloves. Oh, my! The pads were so stiff that I could hardly walk, except in a stiff-legged shuffle. They were those very wide, bulky wicket-keeping pads often seen on the legs of junior and club 'keepers who cannot catch the ball with any confidence, and know that they must use their pads instead of their hands for stopping the ball. I am not criticising any wicket-keepers—good luck to them all— but oversize, bulky pads do not allow for that easy freedom and quick movement that is so essential behind the stumps.

Anyway, so far as that new equipment of mine is concerned, I had to wear it, and out we went to field. As it happened, the opening batsman was the aggressive type. He hit a four off the first ball and then tried to repeat the stroke off the third delivery. The ball soared straight up into the air about mid-wicket. Naturally, I was keen to get after it, and with a yelled " All right ! Leave it to me ! " I dashed down the wicket.

Alas, I had forgotten those huge pads I was wearing. When I had gone only a few yards, I stumbled and fell flat on my face, and the ball dropped with a dull thud about a yard from me.

I scrambled up, with my flannels and shirt badly grass-stained, to find batsmen, fielders and umpires roaring with laughter. I was never so embarrassed in my life. With a muttered " Excuse me ! " to the skipper, I rushed off the field. Once in the pavilion I changed into my old pair of pads, and then unearthed a very worn pair of wicket-keeping gloves. They were slightly threadbare, but I preferred these to the new ones. Then out I went again, feeling much happier—and infinitely more comfortable.

Rutherford, a promising young Australian batsman, receives a nasty crack on the hand from a rising ball when Frank Tyson was bowling at Perth (W. Australia). It shows what the Australian batsmen were up against on their fast wickets.

This picture illustrates Len Hutton's aggressive policy during the last tour of Australia. Brian Statham is bowling to a ring of fielders, and only cover point is out of camera range.

Len Hutton and the author with their wives, Jean Evans (*on left*) and Dorothy Hutton, throwing coins into the Wishing Well at King's Park, Perth, Western

Len Hutton looks on as Frank Chester gives one of his undisputed decisions behind the bowler's wicket. The whole

So, stumpers, whenever you get a new pair of gloves or pads, give them some attention before you attempt to wear them in match play. Gloves, for instance, must be made really pliable. Pull them about, screw them up—treat 'em a bit rough. Put them on your hands and punch your left fist into the palm of the right glove until you have moulded a cup-like hollow. Remember, the ball has got to nestle neatly in the palms of the hands. Do likewise with the other glove.

I have even used the bottom of a bat to punch the newness out of gloves and soften the leather. Pull the fingers about, too. Be careful not to destroy the protective ribbing and padding, of course, but make them pliable enough so that you can move your fingers freely. You should be able to " feel " the ball when you take it in your gloves.

Much the same applies to pads. If you must have a new pair, I suggest you take them into the nets a few times before you wear them in a match. Knock them about a bit, and allow other chaps to use them until they have lost all their new stiffness.

Light pads are the best. After all, a stumper should catch the ball with his gloves, and not be content to stop it with his pads, which should be merely a secondary precaution against knocks. Why not use your ordinary batting pads? When you are batting you must run fast between the wickets, but wicket-keeping calls for pretty swift movement, too, whether it is chasing the ball within reach of the wicket, or dashing back to the stumps to take hasty throw-ins. Remember, too, that no one does more bending or stooping than the 'keeper, and how on earth can you do that if you are wearing stiff, bulky pads?

Equipment is definitely important to the wicket-keeper, so see that yours is easy to wear, and comfortable. Believe me, this is sound advice. I can assure you that I would never wear new equipment in a match. My best pals are my old pads and my well-worn gloves.

I am often asked how I know when to spring up off

my haunches when receiving a ball standing close to the wicket. I can only reply that this action comes automatically to any natural wicket-keeper. If the hands are kept clear of the body, they can move swiftly in the direction of the approaching ball, and, in consequence, can make up for any slight error in timing that may be made in rising from the squatting position. If the hands are held in the correct position, it matters little whether the ball keeps low or gets lift from the pitch, they will move automatically and swiftly to the ball, irrespective of the rise of the body.

Another of the questions so often asked me is this : " Do you rely on signals between the bowler and yourself ? " The answer is—sometimes. Doug Wright and I have a secret code, which he uses when he is going to bowl his faster ball, and I once found it necessary to arrange for Peter Loader to signal to me when he was changing his pace.

It was in a Gentlemen and Players match at Lord's that I first kept wicket to Peter. At a vital stage of the game he puzzled Bill Edrich with his slower ball, and it was snicked behind the wicket. I lunged forward in an effort to catch it, but it did not carry sufficiently, and the chance was missed, merely because I was not ready for any such change of pace on Peter Loader's part.

It was after this incident that Peter and I got together and arranged for him to signal to me whenever he was about to bowl his slower ball.

This is not always necessary, of course, but it does pay dividends sometimes for a wicket-keeper to be given forewarning of any particular type of ball. On the whole, however, it is up to the wicket-keeper to make a study of the bowlers he is called upon to take, and to be concentrating hard enough to take whatever comes. However, if young 'keepers feel that it would give them confidence to receive signals from certain bowlers, then I am all in favour. Confidence means so much in this difficult all-action job of keeping wicket.

So far as I am concerned, standing up to all sorts of

bowling throughout a full English County and Test season is no easy task, believe you me. It calls for one hundred per cent. fitness, strength, and, may I say it, courage, too. The stumper gets many hard knocks that are not obvious even to his fielding colleagues. I know—I've had plenty, especially from those balls on the leg side which hit one on the forearms, on the wrist, on the chest, and even in the teeth sometimes.

I have also had my nose broken a couple of times from balls that flipped up from the batsman's pads. I've even been given a couple of black eyes—and a severe gash—from the bat ! However, those misfortunes are merely sent to try us chaps behind the stumps. It is up to wicket-keepers to be sufficiently wide awake to prevent the ball hitting them—their gloves are for stopping the ball !

Here is a tip for all budding 'keepers. A spirit of bravado is no good behind the stumps, if it means that you are continually off the field with minor injuries. Better to be safe than sorry. But if you get knocks—as you will—then take your blows without making a fuss. Showmanship can so easily be misunderstood. So carry on with your job, or you will have people saying : " He's a poor sort. He can't stand up to the strain." Never let that be said about you.

In conclusion, I have been asked to mention a few of my wicket-keeping contemporaries. There are so many; for the standard of wicket-keeping both in the Counties and in the world of Test cricket continues to make great progress.

It used to be thought that to do his job effectively the wicket-keeper had to be small, neat and compact. I wonder . . . ? Australia has in Gil Langley a stumper whose outlook on his job and on the game in general is similar to mine, yet in my opinion he is one of the most untidy looking 'keepers I have ever seen. However, his ability behind the stumps is in no way minimised by his appearance. He is short and stocky—the ideal build, as a matter of fact, and certainly a worthy cricketer to represent Australia.

On the other hand, so far as stature is concerned, there is John Waite, of South Africa, who must be one of the tallest 'keepers in the game. Yet he did such a fine job behind the stumps during the 1955 season that he must be classed as one of the finest 'keepers ever produced in South Africa.

I must say a word of praise to the now retired Don Tallon. In his prime he was without doubt one of the greatest 'keepers ever to wear the gloves. Don's asset was his quickness of movement once the ball found his gloves, and his anticipation at times was almost uncanny.

Len Maddocks, who took over from Gil Langley when Gil received a blow in the eye in a State match, did so well in the third Test at Melbourne, that he was retained for the fourth at Adelaide, although Gil was then fit again. This created quite a stir among the South Australian cricket public. Maddocks appears so much neater and smarter in appearance than Gil that this may have had some bearing on his choice, although I cannot believe it was so. However, Len's batting ability was certainly a factor in his selection.

So far as wicket-keeping is concerned, it would be difficult to single out the better of the two, but from what I have seen of both men, my own vote would go at the moment to Gil Langley, who sticks to fundamentals in cricket and in life, and says that looks shouldn't matter anyway. Perhaps he's right ! Certainly Australia must be happy in the knowledge that they have two really fine wicket-keepers.

Mention of Len Maddocks recalls an incident that happened in the last Adelaide Test. He and Ian Johnson were putting on some quick runs, and Len, who is a snappy runner between the wickets, played a ball to mid-wicket, where Bob Appleyard was fielding. Len called for a quick single, but Ian Johnson, sizing up the situation in a flash, yelled " No ". Maddocks was stranded in the middle of the pitch as Bob gathered up the ball.

He evidently thought he had time to make sure of a

perfect throw to me, and he gave me a gentle lob. Unfortunately, he misjudged the elevation of his throw, and the ball rose at least three yards above my head, and right out of my reach. Consequently, Len Maddocks made his ground safely, and a grand opportunity was missed of a run-out.

There is a moral here for all fielders. Don't try to be too clever when you throw-in, but react naturally. If Bob Appleyard had gathered the ball and slung it straight at me, Maddocks would have been run out—no doubt about that. Of course, this business of natural reaction and not trying to be too clever, applies not only to the other fielders but also to every phase of the wicket-keeper's work behind the stumps.

Just one other wicket-keeper I would like to mention, and that is Don Brennan, to my mind, one of the finest amateur stumpers of my day. What I liked particularly about the Yorkshireman was his speed once he had the ball in his gloves. There are plenty of wicket-keepers who take the ball cleanly enough but are so slow in their follow-up movements that the batsman is allowed those split seconds to nip back into position before the bails go flying. But no such chances could be taken with Don Brennan.

Unfortunately, he did not enjoy too robust health and I think that may be the reason why he was not given more international chances. On his day he was as good as any in the world, but I know he will forgive me saying that he was not really robust enough for the job of six-days-a-week wicket-keeping.

Best of luck, 'keepers !

CHAPTER XII

Bowlers of All Sorts

I AM CONSTANTLY ASKED FOR MY OPINIONS ON BOWLERS—whom do I think is the fastest bowler in the world today ?—whom do I consider the world's best all-round bowler ?—what do I think of the spin of So-and-So ?—is Wardle better than Lock ?—and numerous other questions.

It is not easy to make decisions, but after reflecting on all the bowlers to whom I have kept wicket and batted against during my career, I have reached these deliberations. Pace bowlers first. I put them in this order—Frank Tyson the fastest—Ray Lindwall the most varied—Brian Statham the straightest—and Keith Miller the most hostile.

When I voice these opinions, most people say : " Ah, yes, but what about Alec Bedser ? "

Well, to my mind, Alec is the best of his type in the world, and I am willing to contest this point with anyone. Alec has been such a great worker since the war that we are apt to forget that he was the mainstay of England's attack when we virtually had no bowlers at all compared with the Australians for instance. When Ray Lindwall and Keith Miller were in their early twenties they had the cricket world at their feet ; in consequence, with such brilliantly hostile bowlers, backed up by magnificent fielding and a rare display of high-powered batting, Australia had a side in 1946 and '48 that conquered the world. At this time, Alec Bedser was England's only pace-man to have any real effect on those superb Australian batsmen. I am firmly convinced that our batsmen, on the whole, were equally as strong and capable as the Australians, but because our bowling was below par and theirs was so much above par, we were fighting what

I can only call a losing battle. I look at it this way. If Neil Harvey, Sir Donald Bradman and the rest of that great array of batsmen had had their own bowling to contend with, I am sure they would not have made so many runs—or so easily. But cricket has always been like that. Supremacy invariably goes in cycles, when one side is better than the other, or one player of a particular class is greater than his counterpart, although of course, such comparisons seldom prove anything.

To return to Alec Bedser. Let me repeat that I regard him as the greatest bowler I have ever played with or against, because, although he has never had the pace of the faster bowlers, he has had the ability, without real pace, to make the ball swing in the air both ways, while his leg-cutter became world famous. Alec rolled his fingers over the ball as he delivered it, and as it swung, it pitched on the seam and became, as it were, a leg-spinner. As it hit the turf, it would cut away sharply and often I have seen Lindsay Hassett, Sir Don Bradman and many other great Test players completely beaten—if not bowled out, by that magnificent ball. And not only the Australians. Alec has puzzled all the best English batsmen with his leg-cutter.

I once saw Denis Compton bowled in a Scarborough Festival match by the same type of ball that dismissed " The Don "—and often caught Arthur Morris in two minds. Yes, Alec has been—and still is—a very great bowler, the best medium pacer I'm ever likely to see. In fact, the best of this age. I know many Sussex cricket lovers will disagree with me. They will contend, with good reason, of course, that their own Maurice Tate was the greatest of that type of bowling. Well, I cannot believe that anybody was better than Alec.

I was speaking to Leslie Ames not so very long ago about this very same thing. Les kept wicket to Maurice and he said he thought that on a hard, fast wicket Maurice Tate was a better bowler than Alec, because he seemed to make the ball come up off the pitch so quickly, and move off the seam so fast that he gave the batsman very little chance of defence. But he agreed that Alec is a better bowler than Maurice on the slow dead type of wicket, because Maurice did not seem to have the ability to make it come off anything like so quickly, and, what is more, he did not have the leg-cutter. On the other hand, Alec has developed his leg-cutter so much that on a slow rather dead wicket he can still make the ball bite, lift, and turn as if he were a spin bowler.

Perhaps it is presumptuous on my part to draw comparisons in this way because I never kept wicket to Maurice Tate except in a war-time match, when he was much slower than in his prime. But I must admit that I was amazed that this rather portly gentleman could make the ball swing and float about in the air so much. That was the only time I kept wicket to Maurice Tate, but I realised then what a great bowler he must have been, for although his age was against him, he still had the ability to make the ball dip and swing. However, I stick to my opinion that Alec Bedser is the greatest medium-pacer of this age.

I am often asked how Alec manages to make the ball cut away once it pitches, and is able to control the swing so well that he makes the ball dip in so late. I cannot give any explanation. It is just a natural ability that he has developed, plus a very rhythmic run up to the wicket. Nowadays it takes Alec a couple of overs to loosen up, but his action is still perfect, he has lost none of his skill, and he retains his enthusiasm for 100 per cent. physical fitness. That is why he is still in the international class despite his years in the game. You know it's a wonderful thing to have a person like Alec Bedser on your side. Although some people contend that he was a failure on the last tour of Australia, I do not agree. I will go further and say that he was really a success. It was partly due to us having Alec as a " reserve " that the Australians were beaten. It had a great psychological effect on the opposition, for they must have thought that if we could keep a bowler of Alec's reputation in reserve, then we had better bowlers than he. Imagine the demoralising effect this must have had upon the Australians.

I admired the philosophical way Alec took all this. His spirit was an inspiration, for I never once heard him utter a word of protest or criticism. In my own mind I felt that he should have played in the last Test, but if he had been selected, it would have been unfair on the players who had done so well in the previous three Tests which we had won. You can't have it both ways !

Now to Frank Tyson—in my opinion the world's fastest bowler. I cannot think of anybody faster—and I have never kept to anybody else of equal pace.

Is he faster than Harold Larwood, the former Notts Test " quickie " ? This question has been asked innumerable times, but it is a question without answer. Personally, I never kept to Harold Larwood, but Leslie Ames did—hundreds of times, and we have often discussed our experiences whilst keeping wicket to the considered fastest bowlers of two eras. Our experiences are very similar.

Les has told me how, when Larwood bowled one wide of the crease—down the leg side to a right-hander, for instance—he had only just time to get across to gather the ball, often at full stretch.

Much the same happens when Frank Tyson is bowling. You may imagine that I make some of my " takes " look more difficult than they are, but I assure you I should not fling myself about, unless I was forced to—and from some of Frank's fastest balls that beat the bat, a full-length dive is my only chance of preventing byes.

On fast wickets I need to stand about twenty yards behind the stumps—or nearly the length of a pitch—to take Frank's expresses. Even then I invariably have to move pretty quickly—but what amazes me is how batsmen cope with them. But then batsmen have always found a way to deal with pace-men—at least, the best of them.

Next on my " honours list " of fast bowlers is Ray Lindwall. A magnificent cricketer, and to my mind, the

almost perfect bowler. Ray is not now so fast as in 1946
and when he came over in '48, of course. He was then
the quickest in the world. I recall the Test at Manchester
in 1948 when Denis Compton was hit over the eye
by a Lindwall bouncer. If you remember, Denis came
back and made a magnificent 134, but Ray really did
bowl very fast indeed at Old Trafford, and I am quite
certain that on that wicket he couldn't have been much
slower than Frank Tyson.

I shall never forget that Test because of one particular
episode concerning Bill Edrich. Now in those days, Bill
was something of a speed merchant and was considered
by most batsmen as a bit of a " slinger ". Bowling to
Ray Lindwall, Bill bounced three in a row. The third
was quite a nasty one, and hit Ray on the arm. Naturally we all clustered round and Bill asked him if he was all
right.

" Yes, I'm all right, Bill," Ray answered, " but you
can't do this to me and get away with it ! "

After that good-natured " threat ", Bill was expecting
a few bouncers when he went out to bat, and, by jove, he
got them !

Ray was definitely " dynamite " when he wanted to be,
but he was " great " because he had the knack of varying
his pace so well. If the bowler has mastery of the surprise
element, which enables him to make the ball leave his
hand faster or slower than appears from his normal action,
then he must keep the batsman guessing. Ray Lindwall's
use of the new ball was wonderful. He kept it well up
to the batsman, made it swing and had such control of
length, direction and variety of pace that he was a menace
to any batting side. I am sure that during my career Ray
has been unsurpassed for all-round bowling excellence.

Now we come to Brian Statham, the straightest pace-
man of them all. I've never known a fast bowler to bowl
so consistently straight as Brian. I should know. The
ball comes through so truly. Brian believes in making
batsmen play at the ball, but when they miss it, and the
ball does not hit the stumps, invariably it flashes past so

close to the wicket that the slips fling their hands in the air, and I, as wicket-keeper, have an appeal on the tip of my tongue. It seems impossible sometimes for the ball to miss the stumps, yet if you study the scores throughout the season, I am certain you will find the words " bowled Statham " so often that it will astound you. I should think he bowls more players than any other contemporary fast bowler because of his uncanny accuracy. His consistency is remarkable.

I have known him bowl for a long spell in the morning, and another long spell in the afternoon, and then come on in the evening for his last spell of the day, perhaps in humid heat, and bowl his first ball right on the mark, absolutely straight. I have known that first ball to come as such a surprise to the batsman that it has taken a wicket. Most batsmen expect a bowler to be stiff after a lengthy break, and, looking for runs, try to swing the first ball round the corner. Often this comes off—but not with Brian Statham, the fast bowler who seldom sends down a loose or misdirected ball.

From accuracy of direction, we go to hostility—and that means Keith Miller. He has such a lovely flowing action, and delivers the ball from his full height with his arm extended, that when he bowls a ball short of a length it is given " lift " that brings the ball chest high to the batsman. Often it moves a little off the seam, too, because Keith has the ability to do that, due to his high action. When it also swings a little in the air before pitching, it is a most difficult ball to play. It is impossible to get out of the way of it. You've got to play it.

I have seen numerous batsmen caught behind the wicket off Keith through playing back to a ball that comes up chest high and just gets the shoulder or the top half of the edge of the bat. A certain catch for wicket-keeper or slips. With menacing " short-legs ", too, a batsman must play the ball dead true, so that it drops straight down, otherwise it's a catch. Yes, Keith is a great bowler, certainly the most hostile I have ever met—and I am sure we have not seen the last of him yet.

So—Frank Tyson, Ray Lindwall, Brian Statham, Keith Miller—but that does not exhaust the really outstanding fast bowlers of my age. A few years ago there was Cuan McCarthy, the South African, who at one time looked as if he would develop into one of the best fast bowlers ever produced in the Union. But as I have told you in a previous chapter, I feel that as a young chap in the early part of his career, he was over-bowled because South Africa were lacking in quick bowlers. He tended to pitch the ball a fraction too short. In consequence, he did not get the wickets he should have done, and was later omitted from the South African team.

When I was speaking to Len Hutton one day, I asked him : " Who do you think, Len, is the fastest bowler you've played against ? "

Len's reply was : " I think Cuan McCarthy is as quick as anyone."

" Do you think he's as quick as Ray Lindwall ? " I asked.

" Yes—at the moment," was the answer, " but perhaps not when Ray was a little younger, in 1946 and '48 for instance."

Coming from Len Hutton that was a great tribute to a young man who promised much, but faded, through no real fault of his own.

Another former Test bowler who troubled English batsmen a few years ago was Jack Cowie from New Zealand. A great-hearted trier who was not as fast as some of his contemporaries, but he was a difficult bowler to score runs against, because he invariably bowled just short of a length, making the ball difficult to get away. He was a similar stamp to our own England and Lancashire bowler Dick Pollard.

Last summer we saw two newcomers to the ranks of Test pace-men in the South Africans Neil Adcock and Peter Heine. When I first saw them I thought Neil was a fraction quicker than Peter, but one has to remember that the latter was a very raw recruit to first-class and international cricket when he arrived in England. He was left out of the first Test at Nottingham but from then on he made great strides, always keen and ever ready to learn. Towards the end of the tour he was, I would say, equally as quick as Neil Adcock, and he developed quite a bit of hostility, too. With his height of six feet four inches, and long arms that enable him to make the ball get up, just short of a length, he is built for fast bowling, and I think he will develop even more and become one of South Africa's attack mainstays of the future.

Neil Adcock was unfortunate, for most of the summer he was hampered by a broken bone in his foot, and, therefore, we did not see the best of him, but he's certainly a prospect for the future.

Before I pass on to other types of bowling, I must not forget some of the youngsters coming along. Freddie Trueman, for instance, a really hostile pace-man, and quite a character in his own way. He is so enthusiastic on the field that he tends to lose some of his self-control, particularly when decisions go against him. This has made him a controversial figure, but I think I know Freddie well enough to realise that he does not mean to make himself objectionable or unpopular. He's out on the field to do his best ; he'll bowl his heart out, and field like a madman, all in the interest of his side. He really does put his heart and soul into his job, and no one can blame him for that, even though he allows his insatiable enthusiasm to run away with his control at times.

Yorkshire also have young Michael Cowan coming along, too. He's a left-arm " quickie " who should go a long way once he gains experience. Les Flavell, of Worcestershire, is also most promising. He impressed me last season when he took nine Kent wickets, a very good performance. He is now quite fast, but I remember when I first saw him he was rather wiry, and did not look particularly strong ; he also had a longish run and flailing arms. But now he has developed a fine physique, he's big, tall and strong, and is getting real power into his bowling.

Well, what of Australia's successors to Ray and Keith ?

One doesn't know, but we did see Pat Crawford, of New South Wales, when we were over there last time, and he is by no means a slow bowler. He is tall, rather wiry I should say, and he's a great trier. I think that Pat will do well in England.

Before I leave fast bowlers, I feel I should say something about one of the most controversial of all modern cricket topics—the no-balling of fast bowlers because of " drag ". It is a subject that is discussed wherever cricket is the topic of conversation, both in this country and in Australia.

Let me say straight away that there should be a definite ruling given to umpires—an unmistakable definition which would enable them to say yes or no in any specific case. At the moment it is left entirely to the umpire himself. One umpire will take his mark from an imaginary line six inches from the bowling crease, another a foot behind it, and so on. The fast bowlers do not know quite where they stand in this matter.

I remember Freddie Trueman's experience at Lord's in a Test match. He was no-balled several times by an umpire, whose idea of " drag " was different from some of the others. His imaginary line was farther away from the crease. This so upset Freddie that he bowled badly. No wonder the big Yorkshireman asked " Why ? "

Ray Lindwall had similar experiences when he first came over here, because the ideas of different umpires were so varied. Ray solved the problem by making his own mark behind the bowling crease, and from then on he was hardly ever no-balled.

To the question of should this be necessary, I say no. If a fast bowler's foot drops behind the line that is already there, then I say it is a fair ball, irrespective of the distance the bowler drags. Some people suggest that the delivery should be a fair one if the bowler's front foot lands inside the space between the two creases—in other words, behind the batting crease. At first glance, this seems to provide the answer, but from first-hand experience, and from the opinions of umpires to whom I have spoken, I do not think it would be practicable. Umpires tell me that they would not have time to call no-ball on the front foot, because the ball has left the hand by the time the front foot is down. Umpires are only human, and they could not be expected to watch the foot and then instantly focus on the ball, which, by then, would nearly have reached the batsman. With such a short time in which to see the ball, it would be practically impossible for an umpire to give accurate l.b.w. decisions that are so essential.

So I contend that the rule concerning the no-ball should be clear cut, to make it legitimate for the bowler to land behind the bowling crease, irrespective of any drag that might follow. We must remember that the no-ball rule was originally instituted for underhand bowling, but although the game itself has progressed and developed to such an extent, the rules are very much the same as they were when the game was in its infancy.

Coming to bowlers of slightly less than express pace, one must not forget Fazal Mahmood, of Pakistan. He proved on his last tour over here that he had not the pace of the others I have mentioned, but rather did he resemble Alec Bedser, in that he was able to bowl a most effective leg-cutter, and swing the ball, too. Talking of the medium-to-fast type of bowler, there was, of course, Bill Johnston, Australia's left-arm exponent of pace. He was about the same pace as Mahmood, but bowling left arm he had the natural ability to deliver a form of pacey " off-spin ". In fact, when the wicket suited him, he often switched from the medium pace fastish ball to the slightly slower off-spinner, and when he did that on a wicket that helped him, Bill Johnston was a very great bowler indeed.

Talking of Johnston reminds me of Hines Johnson, from Jamaica, whom we met during our last trip to the West Indies. He stood about six feet four inches and was tremendously strong, with a rhythmic run-up, but rather an ugly action. However, he had a very good follow-through, and on his day he was certainly a very quick bowler. At the moment the West Indies' fast attack is dependent upon Frank King, who, I think, pitches the ball a fraction too short to be a really great bowler. But if he were to keep the ball up a little more and use the short ball as a surprise instead of as his normal delivery, as he does at the moment, I feel he would improve his bowling considerably.

To return to England for a moment, for a brief mention of several more of our outstanding " quickies ". First of all, there's Peter Loader who, although he did not play in a Test in Australia, was, nevertheless, very successful out there. Peter materially helped us to win the Ashes by taking over in some of the matches as deputy for Frank Tyson and Brian Statham, enabling these two players to take an occasional well-earned rest. But had Peter not bowled so well, these periods of rest for Frank and Brian would have been impossible and their power in the Tests would have been immeasurably lessened.

Make no mistake about it, Peter Loader is a very fine, hostile fast bowler. Off the field, the Surrey bowler is a most friendly fellow indeed, but when he is bowling there is nothing friendly about his attitude to the batsman. His only desire is to get the batsman's wicket and send him back to the pavilion. That's the right approach for any bowler, I think, for too many players are inclined to take things too easily when they are in the field. Peter appears to hate the batsmen, judging by the way he tears into it. He gets really hostile against any batsman who hits him for four. And why not ?

Of course, we could not leave out of this chapter our No. 1 all-rounder in the England side—Trevor Bailey. Trevor has his critics, but he can be a very good asset to any side, for he is a medium pace bowler who can make the ball move off the wicket. He does not swing it so much in the air, but he is very accurate. He takes rather a longish run for a medium pacer, but he tells me that without that run his rhythm would be lost, but once he gets into his natural rhythm, he can more or less deliver the ball exactly where he wants to put it. I have often noticed Trevor's footmarks as he comes up to bowl and invariably they cover an area approximately two feet wide, which means that Trevor delivers the ball from different positions, which automatically makes each delivery slightly different from the previous ball, and, therefore, keeps the batsman guessing.

Trevor is certainly a student of cricket. On the field he is always keenly watching the batsmen, looking for their faults and, once he has discovered the chink in a batsman's armour, he plays on it, often worrying the batsman into a fatal error. Several times in Test matches he has " thought out " Keith Miller, just when the big fellow has looked like getting on top of the bowling. We all know that Keith is never the same player if he is unable to dictate the rate of scoring, and knowing this, Trevor usually concentrates on bowling on the leg stump, with a mid-wicket, when facing Keith. The Australian eventually loses his patience and tries to force strokes off balls that should be left alone. Invariably this ends Keith's innings, and Trevor Bailey has got another wicket. I have seen it happen quite often.

As I write this, I am reminded of another fast bowler to whom I have kept wicket many times—Fred Ridgway, our own Kent pace-man, who was such a power in the County game before illness and injury hampered him during the last season or two. I am certain that Fred had the ability to be a great bowler. Amazing though it may seem, he was able to move the ball *after* it had passed the bat. When I was standing back I have seen the ball coming straight down the wicket, hit the turf, and the batsman has left it alone. Then, all of a sudden, for no accountable reason, the ball has started swinging and floating on its way back to me. There have been occasions when I have let one or two byes go through for that very reason. How Fred got that ability, I do not know. It was a natural asset, I suppose, and if only he could have developed his bowling more, I feel he would have played for England on more occasions than he actually did.

All the Counties today are coming to rely more and more on their fast bowlers, and the standard is approaching that of pre-war days.

12

Well, so much for the fast bowlers, but no team would be very successful without the " spin-sters ", those chaps who are expected to bowl and bowl—and go on bowling. So in fairness to these grand fellows, I feel that we should talk a little about them—the off-spinner, the leg-spinner, the left-arm orthodox bowler, and the left-arm " China-man " and googly bowler. The off-spinner is a ball, which, against a right-hand batsman, pitches outside his off stump and turns towards him. In other words, it breaks from left to right.

Foremost in this class, and an expert, is Australian Ian Johnson. I have already discussed in another chapter. Ian's oft-criticised " throwing " action, because of his bent elbow as he delivers the ball, but as he has not been " no-balled " for doing so, we must presume he does not throw. However, there is no doubt that he has the ability to toss the ball very high in the air, and spin it at the same time. He also has the ability to make it appear that the ball is going to be a half volley, but when the batsman goes out to drive it, he finds it's not quite there. Ian has got a lot of his wickets by enticing batsmen to drive him hard, and then seeing the ball snapped up by alert fielders—because the ball wasn't exactly what it appeared to be.

In England his counterpart, I suppose, is Jim Laker. Now Jim is a really fine bowler, although he has been most unlucky. I have heard the criticism that Jim is inclined to throw in the sponge when he's not getting wickets, but personally I cannot agree with that. Jim may be a little temperamental, I agree, but as a bowler I think he's the " tops " in the off-spin class. Although he is sometimes compared with Bob Appleyard, they are totally different types, for Bob is much faster.

Jim Laker has done grand work for his country. I remember him bowling almost continuously from lunch until tea-time in the final Test against the West Indies in Jamaica, when we needed this match to draw the series. He bowled 30-odd overs for 45 runs and 2 wickets. It was a magnificent spell of bowling, one of the finest I have ever seen from an off-spinner, for Clyde Walcott was batting, and we all know he hits the ball hard—harder, I should think, than any other contemporary player. Jim kept him pegged down and eventually got him caught by Tom Graveney. In view of that wonderful spell of bowling, to say that Jim chucks it in when he's not getting wickets is plain foolish. He only got two in that spell, but he kept going like a hero.

Talking of off-spinners, one must not forget South Africa's Athol Rowan. He was rightly classed as one of the best off-spin bowlers of his time. He has been succeeded by Hughie Tayfield, who has broken most of the records for South Africa, both in England and in Australia. You know, there's something about Hughie that most batsmen cannot quite fathom. We all think we should get after him, to hit him all over the field. When you are at the wicket and you see the ball coming down, you think it's the easiest thing in the world, only to find out your error too late. He has a knack of making that ball drop a fraction shorter than it actually appears to be doing, and, therefore, when you go to drive it, you're not quite there, and the ball rises into the air instead of travelling hard and low. Because of this, Hughie gets a lot of his wickets from catches on the leg-side, at silly mid-on, silly mid-off and by himself as bowler.

If any batsmen can collar bowling, it is usually the Australians, but when South Africa were visiting Australia, nobody really collared Hughie Tayfield. I admit, from the spectators' point of view, he looks a very medium-class bowler, but in actual fact he's a really top-class off-spinner, which is proved by the number of his victims.

A word now about Bob Appleyard. He did a wonderful job in Australia, mainly because of his ability to vary his pace so much. He doesn't spin it a lot : he's rather apt to cut the ball instead of spinning it, and, therefore, unless the wicket is helping him, Bob doesn't really do a lot with the ball. But he is usually very accurate, fairly quick, and that bewildering variation of pace is a great asset to his bowling. He also has one exceptionally good ball, a fast " yorker ". Very difficult to spot, it gets him a lot of wickets. I've noticed this variation sometimes from behind the stumps. The batsman is invariably playing the shots much too soon and, in consequence, is caught.

The off-spinner is a useful asset to a side, because he can be so economical. An off-spinner should be able to go on, and bowl just around the off stump, spinning the ball in to the batsman, particularly if it's a turning wicket. This is run-saving bowling ; what is more it enables the captain to rest his fast bowlers. I am not suggesting, of course, that off-spin need be negative. On the contrary, if the close-to-the-wicket fielding is good, there is always the chance of a wicket. Actually, brilliant close-to-the-wicket fielding can make any off-spinner look much better than he really is, or at least make his bowling more effective.

Young Freddie Titmus, of Middlesex, an up-and-coming all-rounder, who bowls off-spinners, gets many of his wickets from catches in the leg trap.

I find that the standard of the modern off-spinners is much higher than was the case before the war. I think the reason for this is that the new l.b.w. rule has helped the off-spinner. Under the old rule the ball had to pitch *on* the stumps, providing it was going to hit the stumps, of course. Now it can pitch outside the off stump and come back, and as long as your leg is in line and the ball is going to hit the wicket, you are out. This means that batsmen cannot now pad away the off-spinner as in the past, and has materially assisted that type of bowling.

Now shall we have a word about the leg-spinners ? First on my list is my Kent captain, Douglas Wright, who to my mind, is the greatest leg-spinner I have ever seen. In his prime a few years ago he was so much quicker than the other bowlers of his class. He really did spin the ball and bowled a well-concealed googly. Even on the best of wickets, he was able to get the ball to do something. In consequence, when bowling well, he could afford to have three short-legs up for the ball to which the batsman would lunge forward, not knowing whether it was a leg-spinner or a googly. If it was the googly, it doubtless would get the inside edge of the bat and a leg slip or short-leg would take the catch. Another victim to Doug, who in his prime in '46, '47 and '48, was universally acclaimed throughout the cricket world as a leg-spinner in a class of his own.

Leg-spinners are very useful in County cricket, and no doubt the people of Nottingham would agree, for they have a real match-winner in Australian Bruce Dooland. I remember seeing him for the first time during the M.C.C. tour of Australia in 1946, and he impressed us all. But, for some reason or other, he was given few chances in his own country, and he came to Nottingham, where he has been an outstanding success. In 1953 he took 172 wickets ; 196 in 1954 and 150 last summer, proving his consistency on any type of wicket.

Australia's best leg-spinner today is Richie Benaud—in fact he is the only leg-spinner with Test experience. On English wickets, which take spin a little more than those in Australia, he might be quite a success. Of course, Australia also had that " queer " bowler Jack Iverson, who, I understand, has now retired from top-grade cricket. He was rather a freak bowler, being able to spin the ball off the middle finger. A right-hander, he held the ball between the first finger and the third finger and thumb, with the middle finger lying flat against the palm of the hand, under the ball. So whichever way he wanted the ball to turn, he flicked the centre finger out either right or left, and allowed the ball to spin off that finger. In actual fact, it was very difficult to tell whether he was bowling a leg-spinner or an off-spinner. Hence, until the batsmen got used to him, he was a great success in first-class cricket.

Among leg-spinners I must mention Eric Hollies, of Warwickshire, who has reached international standard and has done extraordinarily well throughout his career. Eric does not spin the ball quite so much as Bruce Dooland or Doug Wright, but he is perhaps a little more accurate. He rolls rather than spins the ball, but when the wicket is helpful to him, that roll is quite sufficient to make the ball turn enough to beat the bat, and he takes a tremendous number of wickets.

Then, of course, there is Roly Jenkins, from Worcestershire. He relies to a great extent on spin and flight, tossing the ball very high in the air and allowing it to drop down and spin off the pitch. Well, some of the batsmen did not allow it to drop and Roly sometimes came in for a bit of " hammer ". He still does at times, but Roly is not the sort of chap to worry about that. He goes on spinning it—and getting very valuable wickets.

He was a great success when he toured South Africa in 1948 ; in fact, it seemed as if he would reach a hundred wickets on the tour, which had not been done before in South Africa. He missed his target, but he was our most effective wicket-taker. Roly is a very enthusiastic cricketer, always trying to get the best out of himself. I remember on one occasion, a few years ago, he travelled to Kent to visit Tich Freeman for a chat and advice. At the time Roly was concerned because he felt he was not spinning or flighting the ball, and he knew the man who took over 3,700 wickets with his spin bowling was the best man to put him right. I only mention that to show how keen Roly Jenkins has always been on his bowling, and such enthusiasm has brought its rewards.

With these flighty leg-spinners a wicket-keeper is offered more chances of stumpings, than catches, which is most unusual. When Leslie Ames, way back in 1927, captured the world record of 127 victims in a season, 64 of them were stumpings. Now remember, the star of the Kent attack in those days was Tich Freeman. He was a little leg-spinner who used to toss them high in the air. The batsmen would dash down the wicket, fail to get to the pitch of the ball and there was Les whipping off the bails with the batsmen stranded in midfield. As I have said so often before, I always like keeping to leg-spinners. That is why I have had some degree of success when keeping to Doug Wright, my Kent colleague. He has been a great bowler in his time, although the stumping chances

from his spinners have been far fewer than they would be
with a fellow like Roly Jenkins, because Doug is much
faster through the air, and, therefore, the batsmen have
not the same encouragement to go down the wicket to
him.

To my mind, a swift stumping is one of the greatest
thrills of wicket-keeping, but unfortunately chances of
this nature are getting less. There are so few leg-spinners
in the country today that stumpings, as such, are seldom
seen. More's the pity ! The genuine leg-spinner who
was not afraid to toss the ball into the air, and the batsman dashing down the pitch in an effort to hit the bowler
over his head or over extra cover, seem to have faded
from modern cricket today, which is a great shame.

We come now to the slow left-arm bowlers, that is, the
orthodox men like Johnny Wardle, Jack Young and Tony
Lock. England has seldom lacked a number of good left-
arm bowlers, capable of high Test ranking. Going back
into the past, we had chaps like Frank Woolley, of Kent,
and Hedley Verity, of Yorkshire. Nowadays there is a
left-arm spinner in nearly every County side, but the two
most outstanding are Johnny Wardle and Tony Lock.
Jack Young, unfortunately, is reaching the end of a long
and successful career.

Now Johnny and Tony are both orthodox left-arm
bowlers, but they are totally different in their styles.
Tony Lock is the attacker, determined to bowl the batsman with every ball. In contrast, Johnny Wardle is the
thinker, the quiet mover, bowling to keep the runs down,
and trying always to make the batsman lose concentration,
and force him into fatal error.

Tony Lock is not concerned about a batsman hitting
him for four, although he never disguises his annoyance
about it ! He is far more concerned with the fact that
he did not bowl the batsman out. Johnny, on the other
hand, takes himself to task. " Why did he hit me for
four ? Obviously I didn't pitch it in the right spot.
Right, we'll pitch the next one in the right spot and keep
pitching them there, until he makes a mistake."

I refuse to draw comparisons between them. They are two wonderful assets to have in any touring side, and it is due partially to these two grand cricketers that England are so strong in left-arm bowling today. I often hear it said that it is impossible to play them both in the same team. There may be good reason for this contention, but I feel that under certain circumstances, it is better to play two good 'uns than one good 'un and an " also ran ".

Cricket cannot do without its " spin-sters ", for once the pacers and the medium pacers have bowled the shine off the ball, it is the off-spinners and the left-armers who have to do the donkey work and keep the runs down.

We have practically completed our bowling types, except for those left-armers who bowl the " Chinaman " and the googly. The " Chinaman " is a ball bowled by a left-armer that pitches outside the off stump and goes into the bat. It is the leg-spinner's action performed with the left arm. The googly, of course, is the ball, whether it be right- or left-handed, that appears to be turning one way, but in actual fact goes the other.

There are quite a few bowlers with the ability to bowl these two balls. Johnny Wardle mixes an occasional " Chinaman " and a googly with his orthodox deliveries, and does extraordinarily well. He has bowled them in Test matches, and they have paid off, particularly against the tail-enders. Knowing that the lower batsmen like to " have a go ", he tosses the ball up, spins it out of the back of the hand, enticing them to hit it right out of the ground. Down the wicket they go, bat lifted, and down comes the bat—but because of its spin and its deceptive flight, the ball isn't there, and the wicket-keeper has another victim to his credit.

The first of these very useful bowlers was, I think, an Australian named Fleetwood-Smith. He was a great exponent of the " Chinaman ", and the googly, and when he came to England in 1938, he put up some fantastic performances, for his type of bowling was—and still is— very difficult to play effectively.

Denis Compton has bowled the " Chinaman " and the googly, and not without some success. Originally, Denis bowled left-arm orthodox, but he mastered the art of the " Chinaman " and googly to such good effect that he has taken a good many wickets in County cricket. He has had occasional successes in Test cricket, too. I remember at Lord's, against Australia in 1953, how, when we needed a wicket very badly, Len Hutton put Denis on for one over. Lo and behold, Arthur Morris tried to sweep his " Chinaman " to leg, but only skied it and was caught out. That was a valuable wicket indeed, for it gave us a good start, so important in all games.

During my career I suppose I have kept wicket to every type of bowling in the cricket book. It is no exaggeration to say that I know as much about bowling as any man in the game—well, it's my job to know bowlers and bowling. Naturally, I have certain preferences, and, of course, some dislikes.

Speaking as a wicket-keeper, it may interest you to know that I enjoy keeping to a man of Alec Bedser's type, standing up to him. He keeps the stumper right on his toes, for one never knows when a chance for a victim is coming out of the blue. I like a good leg-spinner, too, Doug Wright, my Kent captain, for instance, on his top form. Opportunities are greater from his type of bowling than from any other. There is never any time to relax when a leg-spinner is bowling.

The off-spinner is a different matter, particularly on a worn pitch. Why? Well, the good off-spin ball is usually a half-volley. The batsman steps out to drive, and as the ball turns, the wicket-keeper's view of it is completely obscured. If the batsman misses, as often happens, the ball comes up between bat and pad, perhaps just missing the leg stump, or just over the middle stump, and the time between the stumper getting another view of the ball and it reaching him is so short, that oft-times he is left stranded, with no chance of getting across to it.

I should say that more stumpings are missed off a

bowler of Jim Laker's type than from any other, for the reason I have stated.

What of fast bowling? I enjoy it, especially if it is accurate. Remember, the wicket-keeper standing well back gets a very good view of the ball as it passes—or leaves—the bat. Swift reaction and speed of movement do the rest. . . .

Well, there it is. Now you know my opinions about bowlers. But let me assure you that I am glad I took up wicket-keeping and not bowling—especially fast bowling!

CHAPTER XIII

Batting and Batsmen as I see Them

HAVING WRITTEN A CHAPTER ON BOWLERS, I FEEL I should now devote a few words to the batsmen, for I have now stood behind all the world's leading run-getters since the war.

Although comparisons in this important phase of cricket very difficult, so far as run-getting records are concerned, I can tell you of certain differences in the make-up of the great batsmen behind whom I have had the pleasure of keeping wicket. For instance, Sir Donald Bradman had a totally different outlook from a man like Denis Compton.

The Don's policy was cold, calculated ruthlessness. He went out to hit the ball as hard and as often as possible, without giving the bowler even half a chance of getting his wicket. To prove this point, way back in 1930, at Lord's, Bradman had scored 254 against England when he drove a ball hard and low towards Percy Chapman, fielding at silly mid-off. Percy dived and held a magnificent catch. When the Don arrived in the dressing-room his first remark was :

" Well, what do you know ? The first time I lift the ball off the ground, I'm out ! "

That remark, from a man who had just scored 254, shows the utter ruthlessness with which he tackled his duties as a batsman. His concentration was tremendous, yet he was always icily cool in every way. The Don never seemed to sweat, even when the temperatures were in the 100's—and his score was in the 200's.

How unlike Denis Compton, who is usually bathed in perspiration even when he has been at the wicket only a short while. Watch him keep flicking the sweat out of his eyes as he shapes for the next ball. I know when I am keeping wicket in very hot weather, my one dread is to have a bead of perspiration drip in my eye as the bowler is about to deliver the ball. The same applies to some batsmen, for nothing is more likely to upset their concentration. Yet the really great players, men like Don Bradman, for example, seem somehow to be able to avoid the mistake of allowing their concentration to be broken by little incidents of that nature.

I remember playing in a Gentlemen v. Players match, at Lord's, when Walter Hammond was batting. As the ball was in flight towards him, two pigeons flew directly behind the bowler's arm. Wally immediately stepped away from the wicket and allowed the ball to hit the stumps. He was not out, of course, but his instantaneous reaction showed that Wally had the type of concentration that makes a batsman great. Many a lesser batsman would have made some effort to play that ball, despite the distraction caused by the pigeons.

I feel that too many batsmen today fail to some degree because they allow their concentration to be broken by some minor incident, and, in consequence, lose their wicket.

Our greatest batsman today, from the point of view of concentration, is undoubtedly Len Hutton. It is his ability to be able to set his mind completely on the job in hand, to the exclusion of all else, that makes him so great. I remember batting with him when he scored 200 in the final Test in Jamaica on our last trip to the West Indies. We needed runs so badly to draw level in the series, and the situation was indeed tense, yet several times during our partnership, Len walked down the wicket to me and said :

" Stick it out, Godfrey—you're doing fine ! "

If only I could have shown the same consistency of concentration ; for although I stayed at the wicket for something like 2¾ hours, my longest Test innings, incidentally, I was eventually caught in the deep with my score at 28, purely because I lost my concentration for a few seconds. One realises when batting at the other end

to a master like Len Hutton, how difficult this art of concentration really is.   On one occasion during his wonderful innings, the ball beat Len.   Did he look up and
smile in relief?   Not a bit.   His air of grim determination must have given the bowler the impression that he
was thinking " That won't happen again ! " and that is
no encouragement whatever to the bowler.

There is another form of this ruthless attitude that the
really great batsman must have, or perhaps it would be
better to call it ruthless courage.   I recall that fantastic
innings of Dudley Nourse, when he scored 208 at Nottingham under adverse conditions and batting with a
broken thumb.   Never for a moment did he allow either
the conditions or the pain from his injured hand to affect
his concentration.   It was sheer courage and determination that kept Dudley going.

Peter May will become one of the world's illustrious
batsmen because he has the same psychological outlook.
I first remember playing against Peter when Kent met
the United Services, at Gillingham, a few years ago.
Peter was out for nought to Doug Wright in the first
innings, but such was his determination that he said to his
team-mates : " I'm going to hit this chap Wright for six
in the second innings ! "   True to his word, Peter's first
scoring shot in the next innings was a " six " over the
square-leg boundary off Doug Wright.

Today, Peter May is the best straight driver in the
game.   During his hundred in the Test at Sydney, and
his 91 at Melbourne, the number of times the ball was
driven straight back past Ray Lindwall like a rocket was
something I had not seen in years of Test cricket.   Another
of his favourite shots is forcing the ball wide of cover's
right hand off the back foot, a brilliant scoring stroke.
Yet it is true to say that he has many times been dismissed off this particular stroke, when the ball has lifted,
and he has given wicket-keeper or slips a catch.   But like
all great batsmen, he has never cut out the shot that has
brought him so many runs.

In this connection, think of Denis Compton and his

sweep to leg.   Look at the number of runs he scores from it, even though it does get him out at times.   But to start cutting out those beautiful flowing strokes because of an odd dismissal would spoil the game, and would make for unattractive batting.   There is nothing more exhilarating than playing a shot in which danger lies, and succeeding with it.

Keith Miller is another character who is full of unpredictable strokes which, when they come off, make him as great a player as you could wish to see.   Oozing personality in whatever he does, Keith says : " I'm a public entertainer."   How right he is, and how many cricketers could adopt that same attitude to the game.

Colin Cowdrey of the younger generation, with his rather portly figure, almost reminds me of Walter Hammond.   He reflects the same grace of stroke, and, indeed, plays many of Wally's shots.   One can also say that Colin's temperament is superb in a crisis, and it is in his favour that he is always willing to learn, and to seek advice when things are not going as well as he would wish them to go.

Known to us all as " Kipper ", he has confided in me on many occasions of his apparent inability to get the ball away and score runs.   " I don't know what's wrong today, Godfrey.   I don't seem able to get the ball away."

As I have said to him on such occasions, this is most probably caused through his timing being a fraction out. Then again, there have been occasions when Colin has not been feeling too well, and that may have accounted for some of his lapses into slow scoring during the past year or so.   However, so long as a young player appreciates his failings and his difficulties, then they can be overcome.

I have now mentioned some of the great batsmen of my time.   Each has his own policy, varied though they may be, and each, in his own way, must be right, for individual character moulds a man's own particular style of batsmanship.

The one exception to this rule seems to be Neil Harvey,

whose mode of batting reveals nothing extraordinary. A quiet, reserved man who seldom speaks at the wicket—unlike some I could name who are always chatting in between strokes, Neil's flair with the willow makes cricket lovers both praise and abhor him at the same time. His flashing blade has given me many anxious moments behind the stumps, but I think I have caught him more times on the leg-side than any other player I can remember. His method of playing shots whilst attacking the bowling, makes Neil Harvey one of the most entertaining batsmen of this era. Combined with his wonderful fielding, he certainly is a colourful character on the cricket field. He is a great favourite in his own country.

So was Arthur Morris—but he played his cricket in a different way. He was always ready for a smile and a chat with everyone, whether at the wicket or in the pavilion. He had that same ability to be ruthless when he was batting, but in a rather friendly way, and in so doing, made himself very popular with his own side, and with the opposition, too. It is with regret that we hear of his retirement, for we players and spectators in England will miss this very cheerful character and great cricketer.

There are many more batsmen I could mention here, yet many of these have not attained the degree of fame one would have expected of them judged on their best form. One comes to mind in Joe Hardstaff, Junior, of Notts. I saw him before the war at Canterbury, hit up a really brilliant hundred in only 51 minutes. It was the fastest century of the season, and I never wish to see a better innings. Yet Joe never really produced comparable form in international cricket.

I recall, too, Tom Graveney's 111 in the fifth Test, at Sydney, on the last tour of Australia. Technically it was a beautifully played innings, and a delight for all who saw it, but as the Ashes were already in our hands, it did not carry the same weight of impression because the tension was missing.

Yet it takes all sorts to make a batting side, and such players are needed to make up the teams to represent

County, State or Country, for they help to give life and colour to the game, if so often too infrequently.

In conclusion, I will not produce a list of batsmen in the order of their greatness—that would be well-nigh impossible because our own personal standards differ so greatly, but I would like to name the batsmen who have given me most pleasure.

Among orthodox batsmen there are Sir Donald Bradman, Walter Hammond, Len Hutton, Denis Compton, Dudley Nourse, Peter May and Colin Cowdrey, and the three " W's " from the West Indies—Weeks, Worrell and Walcott.

The left-handers—Neil Harvey, Bert Sutcliffe, Arthur Morris, and Willie Watson in his form of the 1953–54 West Indies tour.

Then come Joe Hardstaff, Tom Graveney, Keith Miller, Vinoo Mankad, and Hanif Mohammad, with Trevor Bailey on defence in a crisis during a vital Test.

There is one other point I want to discuss before I leave batting and batsmen. It concerns England's opening batsmen during the past few years. I am often asked why we are apparently so short of first-class opening batsmen of Test standard. Well, I feel this question can be answered in several ways.

1. The opening bowling of today is so much better than it was immediately after the war.

2. The groundsmen, under instructions from the M.C.C., have cut down the amount of preparation normally given to wickets, and this has provided bowlers with much more chance than they had before.

3. The bowling today has become so much more accurate with the development of swing and pace in most County attacks.

4. The general direction of bowling now tends to attack the leg-side, which cuts down the scoring shots of the batsmen, and, in consequence, opening partnerships are much smaller than when the attack was directed to the off-side, as was the case before the new l.b.w. rule came into being.

It is quite true to say that we have not had an established opening pair since the days of Len Hutton and Cyril Washbrook, but I have no doubt that a new partnership will arise as some of our younger No. 1 and 2 batsmen gain the necessary experience of big-match cricket. Just as we found the men to meet our needs in fast bowling, so will it be with the establishment of a new opening batting partnership, but it may take time.

CHAPTER XIV

My Captains in County and Test Cricket

DURING MY YEARS AS A FIRST-CLASS CRICKETER, I HAVE played under many captains, both for Kent and on Test fields. No two were alike, for each had his own ideas on captaincy and leadership. In fact, as I recall " my skippers ", I realise, on reflection, how different each was from the other.

Let's look first at the Kent captains under whom I have played. When I made my early appearances in the County side before the war, F. G. H. Chalk was skipper. He was a charming fellow both on and off the field, a fine cricketer, too, and everyone in Kent mourned his loss when he was killed whilst on operations as a fighter-pilot with the R.A.F.

Fortunately we had a worthy successor in Brian Valentine, who won the M.C. on Active Service, and took over the Kent captaincy in 1946. He was a jovial character and a very great cricketer indeed, but he retired all too quickly. I shall always remember him telling us that he was relinquishing the captaincy—because he thought it was time he got down to some work. What a laugh that gave us—but Brian was not joking and he handed over to another popular chap in David Clark.

David was not such a good cricketer as his predecessor, but he had a very fine record for the Minor Counties XI, and as a whole-hearted trier he could not be surpassed, but when he opened the innings we never quite knew whether it was going to be a " first baller " or a " half-hourer ". The ability was not quite there, yet David put his back into the job and never gave way.

As a team we admired him very much for his enthusiasm. He handed over to Bill Murray Wood, another young player who was with the County for some considerable time before his opportunity came to captain Kent. His short term of leadership ended in a controversial manner. Some weeks before the end of his second season in that capacity, he was asked to stand down in favour of Douglas Wright.

It is none of my business, of course, but I do feel that the County were wrong in their action. We all knew Bill was not a great captain, and the County did not fare very well under his leadership, but that was not all the skipper's fault. I still contend that the Committee's handling of the situation was not very diplomatic. As a matter of fact, as one of the senior professionals, I did not know what had happened until told by the captain himself that he had been dismissed.

The whole matter received considerable publicity in the Press, which did not reflect much credit on the County. Bill Murray Wood had been captain for one season, and was re-elected for the following year, so I feel that at least the Committee should have waited until the end of the season, instead of dispensing with his services three-quarters of the way through it, particularly during the Canterbury Festival, which is, as you know, every Kent supporter's Mecca.

At the end of the Bill Murray Wood episode, Douglas Wright was appointed skipper—the first professional captain of a Kent side. Doug is still our captain and he has done very well, although I voice it as my own personal opinion that he is rather on the cautious side, and refuses to take risks. Under his leadership Kent have done as well as can be expected with the players we have. But if only we could find another couple of batsmen like Colin Cowdrey and perhaps another opening bowler like Fred Ridgway, who was ill for most of last summer with duodenal ulcers, and some close-to-the-wicket fielders, I think the Kent side would be in the first half dozen again in the Championship. At the moment we are suffering from rather limited playing resources, and I am afraid the County supporter is a little disappointed with us. I don't really blame him, but there just is not the talent in the county.   I wonder why ?   Before the war, Kent were always in the first six, and there were good players to spare.

However, this chapter is about captains, so let me get back to it and discuss now the skippers under whom I have played my Test cricket.

The first was the great Wally Hammond.   I was privileged to be with him in Australia in 1946–47 and also in England several times before he retired, and his vice-captain at that time was Norman Yardley from York-shire.   Each was a fine leader, respected by us all because of his outstanding cricket brain.   Then came F. G. Mann, from Middlesex, a very young captain, who skippered the side to South Africa in 1948 and led a very successful tour.   We won the Test series, and were unbeaten.

George Mann was the son of Frank Mann, who also captained an M.C.C. touring side to South Africa many years ago.   He certainly loved the game, and I often remember him fielding, usually at mid-off when he was captain, and diving full length to stop a ball going for the boundary, rather like Jackie McGlew last summer. George Mann took with him a young team to South Africa and it was his undoubted enthusiasm for the game and his obvious enjoyment of it, rather than his know-ledge and skill as captain, that won the hearts of the young tourists and created a very fine fielding side.   The South Africans were delighted with our side in 1948, and were good enough to tell us that it was the best fielding side they had seen out there.   But I have no hesitation in stating that it was mainly George Mann's influence that made us such a strong combination.

My next Test skipper was that wonderful character F. R. Brown, to my mind, the ideal captain.   A grand cricketer—few better—and a man who went out of his way to understand the players under his command.   He never seemed to mind what we did off the field so long as we were fit to play when called upon and did our best at all times.   Freddie's policy was to allow the lads to behave naturally, knowing that they would do nothing to disgrace him or the team. Because of this policy, I think he got more out of the whole team than possibly any other captain I have known. Although he took to Australia in 1950–51 what most critics said was a weak side, it was through his influence and his understanding leadership that we were praised for putting up a better performance than anyone considered possible. The team just was not strong enough to win the Ashes, but that was not his fault. At the age of 40, Freddie did a jolly good job.

After Freddie Brown, the M.C.C. appointed a professional captain, Len Hutton, who immediately became a most controversial figure in the pubs, clubs and pavilions throughout the country. Well, to my mind, Len was the greatest captain I had the pleasure of playing under, that is from the point of view of policy and strategy. A man with an amazing cricket brain, Len knew what he wanted, and had the courage to stick to his own policies.

He took over the captain's onerous duties when Australia visited us in 1953, and, as you know, we won the Ashes. He retained the position the following winter when we toured the West Indies, and enhanced his reputation as a man of calm courage and deep resolve, for it was indeed a most difficult tour from every aspect.

In 1954 it was the turn of Pakistan to visit Britain, and Len continued his record of never losing a Test series as captain of England. Yet the Yorkshireman was still not without his critics, and prior to the 1954–55 tour of Australia and New Zealand there was considerable controversy about the selection of captain of the M.C.C. party. Should Len Hutton be allowed to continue to hold the position, and thus become the first professional ever to lead the M.C.C. in Australia ? Or should the selection be made from among the several amateurs who were being tipped for the tour leadership—men like David Sheppard, Reg Simpson and possibly Trevor Bailey ?

I remember being asked many times for my own opinion, and without hesitation I always answered : " I am quite certain we will not bring back the Ashes unless Len Hutton goes as captain."

As you know, Len was chosen as skipper and we brought back the Ashes. I would not dare to say " I told you so ", but on reflection I am more sure than ever that if anyone else had been captain—professional or amateur—we should not have retained the Ashes.

In saying this, I am not taking a pro-professional or anti-amateur attitude, for in my opinion, if there was a professional and an amateur of equal capabilities, both as leader and in performance on the field, then I would always plump for the amateur.

I base this contention mainly on the fact that with no financial interest in the game, the amateur is able to carry on in his own way without favouritism or bias. Now I do not wish to be misunderstood, for let me state quite definitely that I do not agree with certain sections of the cricket public who believe that a professional captain is inclined to show favouritism towards his own particular professional friends and colleagues. As a selector, say these critics, he might put forward the claims of one player in preference to another of perhaps superior ability —" the old pals act ", in other words. There are other people who believe that a professional captain cannot have the same control over his fellow professionals as an amateur would have, nor would he speak his mind to the same extent, without fear or favour, thereby doing harm to the whole team.

I would not deny that this *could* happen, but I have never seen any evidence of it. Frankly, I see no reason why a professional cannot handle any situation as well as an amateur captain. As leader of the side he obviously wants the best team possible to lead on the field, so there can be no question of privilege or prejudice. It is quite certain—I repeat, quite certain—that in Len Hutton we had an outstanding example of a man who spoke his mind without fear or favour, if such plain speaking was in the interest of the side, and stood by his decisions, whatever the result.

As I have told you in my chapter dealing with the last tour in Australia, Len suffered considerably at times with back trouble. Last summer, as you all know, that trouble developed so much that he was practically lost to cricket for the season, and then, when we all hoped that he would recover sufficiently to return to the game, came the news that Len had decided to retire from active cricket on medical advice. What a sad blow to Yorkshire—and to England.

When Len had to give up the Test captaincy, there was considerable discussion about his successor. The M.C.C.'s choice fell upon one of our youngest cricketers— Peter May. The choice proved a good one, for Peter has already made his mark as a great batsman, and as a very courageous captain. I think Peter learned a tremendous lot about the job whilst serving under Len on the West Indies and Australian tours, and I am sure that with the experience he has gained under Len, and as skipper against South Africa last summer, he will be England's captain for many years to come.

Among the other captains I have played under, was G. O. Allen, who led us in the West Indies in 1947. At the age of 45, he was past his peak at the time, but still had a very fine action indeed. As I watched him bowling, I could see that when he was a younger man he must have been very fast indeed. Les Ames has often told me that when Gubby Allen was in his prime he was as awkward and as fast as the fabulous Harold Larwood. Well I never played against Harold Larwood so I cannot compare them, but anyway, I saw enough of Gubby Allen to appreciate all the praise I had heard of him. Under his leadership we had a very successful tour of the West Indies even though we did not win a match.

I have also played in teams led by Trevor Bailey and Denis Compton, and one or two others, but I am often asked : " Who would you really like to play under if you had your choice ? " There are several, actually, but the man who comes most readily to my mind is R. W. V. Robins. As a skipper " Robbie " had a sense of humour, and the sort of outlook that made his players feel they were always " in the game ", no matter what the conditions or the score.   His policy was to attack, and to give the batsmen a chance to get runs—and get results.   But then he thoroughly enjoyed his cricket, and wanted everyone else to share in that enjoyment.

A. B. Sellers was another great character under whom I should like to have played.   Not knowing him as well as I do R. W. V. Robins, I may be sticking my neck out, when I say that I think he was a man who said what he thought—without fear or favour—and meant it.   On the field he was the boss, but off the field he was always ready to join in the fun.   Stuart Surridge, of Surrey, is another man under whom I am sure I should have enjoyed playing. I admire his pluck and persistence.   He is not an outstanding performer with the bat, but his close-to-the-wicket fielding and his whole-hearted enthusiasm has virtually made Surrey into a world-beating side.

I must admit too, that I would dearly like to play cricket with Keith Miller as my captain.   He is the type of chap who intrigues me.   He has an uncanny knack of going on to bowl and getting a quick wicket.   It is just as though he has some magical influence which enables him to become something of a super bowler at these times. He seems to instil that spirit into the rest of the team when he is captain.   On our last tour " Down under ", the only State side to beat us was New South Wales, and Keith Miller was captain.   He told me that the New South Wales XI was probably stronger than Australia's Test side, because they played as a team and not as a set of individuals.   I think Keith had something there ! Although I am sure Keith's captaincy had much to do with it.

I would certainly have enjoyed playing under the captaincy of Leslie Ames, whose knowledge of cricket is so vast that I am sure he would have been captain of Kent in the later years of his career.   But owing to his painful back trouble (lumbago, fibrositis, a slipped disc, or whatever the doctors now call this uncomfortable form of complaint that seems to be so prevalent among sportsmen) this pleasure was denied him—and Kent. It was a great pity, for I am certain that if Les had been captain of Kent, his extensive experience and his inspiring influence would have proved invaluable to the County during the lean years of the post-war era.

One other captain deserves mention here, Jack Cheetham, skipper of last summer's South African tourists. From what I saw and heard about him, I should say he had the ideal outlook and approach for a touring captain—in addition to being a grand cricketer. He had a firm control over his players and expected them to keep on top form and give of their best, but he did not hold any hard and fast disciplinary ideas so far as their leisure time was concerned, relying on their loyalty, integrity and common sense to uphold the prestige of South African cricket. In this way he earned their respect, and they responded with their full co-operation.

That is how it should be. I have seen enough of captains to know that the man who shows an appreciation and understanding of his players, will get far more out of them than the dominating, martinet type of leader. After all, players selected to play for England are—or should be—men of responsibility and sense of loyalty to their captain, their colleagues and to the country they represent. They are not children, to be ordered to bed at a certain time, told where to go during their leisure time—and where not to go. Oh, yes, you may not believe it, but this sort of thing has gone on. . . .

From my experience I can assure you that M.C.C. players overseas are sufficiently well disciplined—personally disciplined, I mean—not to disgrace themselves. I have always regarded myself on my many trips to the Commonwealth as an ambassador. If I disgraced myself, I disgraced the whole side—and my country. The right captain encourages the right spirit. He does not need to enforce it.

CHAPTER XV

Hats Off to the Umpires !

CRICKET, AS YOU KNOW, IS GOVERNED ON THE FIELD BY two white-coated gentlemen, who are in sole control of every game played. Their place in cricket is very important, and their decisions vital, for the umpires can make or mar any game, whether it be Club, County or Test match. These decisions can have a great bearing on the result of the match, and for that reason there is no place in cricket for bad umpiring.

Bad decisions are given I know, and umpires are roundly criticised, but much of this is most unjust. I have had the privilege of playing in all parts of the world, and have experienced umpires of various nationalities, and let me assure you that these white-coated gentlemen have always had my sympathy. As a whole, their job is far more difficult than that of the players, yet the majority of them carry out their duties with such thoroughness and efficiency that it leaves me breathless.

When inclined to voice criticism of the umpire, we must not forget that the decision he gives is HIS decision, as he sees the incident. This may mean that the decision is an incorrect one from the point of view of the players, and the spectators, but remember, he makes it from his angle, which is something we are so ready to forget. Many times I catch a batsman behind the stumps and am absolutely positive that the batsman has hit the ball, only to have my appeal turned down by the umpire. The decision is wrong, and we know it, yet it is unfair to condemn the umpire. He gives the decision from his own angle of the incident.

I have spoken to umpires on this matter. The answer has usually been that the umpire saw no deflection of the ball as it left the bat. Quite understandable, for remember, he is standing twenty-two yards from the batsman. Or it may be that there is a wind blowing from behind him, and the faint click of ball meeting bat does not carry to his ears. So when the umpire gives a negative to my appeal, he is correct—from his own viewpoint.

I must admit that I am often dismayed at umpiring decisions, yet I should be the last to offer condemnation or criticism. I know that every umpire I have played with has been fair in his decisions, even though these have not always agreed with my own opinions. The umpires' task is an unenviable one, but there is no question about their ability and knowledge of the game, for many of them have been first-class players, and the experience thus gained is invaluable.

The greatest of all umpires of my time—and I think I have seen them all—was undoubtedly Frank Chester. Frank never claimed to be infallible, yet I am convinced that he made fewer mistakes than any of his colleagues. I have often chatted to him after the day's play about catches he has disallowed, or doubtful l.b.w. decisions, and he has always given me a straight explanation.

I never knew him object to any question I asked ; in fact he told me once that he always pays far more attention to appeals from wicket-keepers and bowlers than from other fielders, because they are the only ones in position to see the incidents. He has, however, taken objection to the angry glances flashed at him by slips and other fielders when he has refused their appeals when they have been in no true position to view the incident for which the request has been made.

Frank Chester was indeed master of his job, and was greatly loved and respected by all touring teams to this country. We were all sorry to hear that poor health has caused him to retire, but he does so with the knowledge that his name will be a byword throughout the cricket world for years to come, and his example will be one that all future umpires will want to emulate.

In Australia all umpires have to pass a theory examination, and are not accepted unless they pass with at least seventy per cent. marks. This is not the ideal way of appointing umpires, of course, but I feel it is paying dividends, for today, Australian umpiring is very nearly the best in the world. On my three tours of Australia, the Press out there have, I feel, been very unfair in their criticism of their own umpires. I can honestly say that there have been fewer mistakes made in Australia than in England during the post-war Test series.

Things are a little different in the West Indies, where umpires do not get the experience afforded to their English counterparts who are officiating in matches every day throughout our County seasons. Is it any wonder then that mistakes are more prevalent in the West Indies ? Umpires out there definitely have my sympathy.

Do you remember the incident I related in my chapter on our last West Indies tour, when an umpire who gave an l.b.w. decision against one of the home batsmen when he was 96, had his wife assaulted on the ground, his father knocked about at work, and his young son thrown into a pond on his way to school ? It was an umpire's decision that started the riots in British Guiana—a very correct decision, too.

Incidents such as these do no credit to the game, for they destroy all efforts at good umpiring. It is difficult to remain completely unbiassed when you know that a decision will bring such unpleasant repercussions.

In the main, however, I have found all umpires fair and just in their decisions. They all make mistakes because they are only human—and we players make plenty, I can assure you of that, too. I have every faith in them, for I know that they will give a just decision, whether it be right or wrong according to my own judgment. So I say—hats off to the umpires !

One thing I would like to see, and that is a panel of neutral Test match umpires. By this I mean—South Africans or Australians in control when we meet the West Indies, for instance, or, conversely, two English umpires when Australia, South Africa or the West Indies are in Test conflict with any country other than England, rather like the neutral referee principle in Soccer inter-nationals.

This matter has already been discussed, I understand, but whether it will ever come only time will tell. Person-ally, I feel that such a system of umpire exchange would be a good thing for cricket in general, because it would obviate the occasional complaint about decisions being biased—although, of course, those of us who have first-hand knowledge of international cricket know that this is completely without foundation. However, it might be worth trying.

CHAPTER XVI

Should Wives Go on Tour ?

MUCH HAS BEEN WRITTEN DURING THE LAST YEAR OR two on the pros and cons of allowing wives to accompany their husbands on tour. I have been asked many times for my personal opinions, so here is an opportunity for me to state my views on this controversial subject.

I am definitely in favour of wives joining their husbands, at least for part of a tour. You may not believe it, but most players suffer from home-sickness in some degree during a tour, and this must have some effect on their play. For this reason alone I believe it is in the interests of the players that wives should be allowed to join them, providing, of course, that the M.C.C. give their permission.

As you know, Len Hutton and I were joined by our wives both in the West Indies and in Australia, and I am quite sure we both benefited by these reunions so far from home. As for the wives, I know I speak for them when I say that they thoroughly enjoyed the experience.

Both in Jamaica, which they reached towards the end of our West Indies tour, and in Australia and New Zealand, they were treated right royally wherever they went. Their only disappointment was that they could not see more of Australia. You see, they were just leaving Colombo when we won the Ashes at Adelaide, and heard the result on the ship's broadcasting system.

They joined us in Melbourne, where we were playing a State match, and then accompanied us to the Final Test at Sydney. Unfortunately the arrival of Jean and Dorothy coincided with a rainy spell, which not only interfered with the two matches, but also prevented them seeing the true beauty of Melbourne and Sydney. Nevertheless, they would not have missed the visit for anything.

Jean and Dorothy made many friends ; in fact it is true

to say that they had very little time to themselves during their short stay in both Australia and New Zealand, because the visit of a Test player's wife is so unusual that she is invited to many of the various social functions arranged for the team and their friends, which enables her to get around far more than might be the case with an ordinary tourist, and allows her to meet and to get to know the people with whom her husband is living during the tour.

Although this almost continual round of entertainment proved something of a strain to our womenfolk, they were able to learn quite a lot about the life of the people in Australia and New Zealand, and it was a memorable experience for them.

Travel broadens the mind and enables one to understand the other man's—and woman's—point of view, so why shouldn't our wives be allowed to enjoy some of the educative experience which is afforded to us ?

However, I am afraid I have deviated slightly from the point—which is to state my views on the question of wives accompanying their husbands on cricket tours.

Let me repeat—it is definitely an advantage to any player to know that his wife will be joining him during the tour. I remember Denis Compton's wife Valerie joining him in Barbados during the last West Indies tour. That was before my wife Jean and Len Hutton's wife Dorothy arrived. Before Valerie's arrival, Denis was not quite his usual self, but her presence made a great difference to him—and to his play. He became the real Denis Compton again.

Not only that, but her arrival created a tremendous good feeling among the people out there, and did untold good for the M.C.C. team as a whole.

In view of all this, I feel that something should be done to make it possible for wives to join their husbands on tour, if only to off-set in some way the major expense of the fare. So far as the expenses incurred by a wife when she reaches the country in which the team is touring are concerned, that is entirely up to the player himself. In this connection, some of the hotels are kind enough to offer special terms and concessions, others are not so generous, but, after all, that is entirely the player's own business. The fare to and from the country of the tour is a very different matter, however.

The M.C.C. have never refused permission, so far as I know, for any wife to join her husband on tour, but they would take no responsibility for travel arrangements or expenses. I do not suggest for one moment that this is a wrong approach, but I do feel that something should be done about it.

After all, there are players who would be only too pleased to have their wives join them on tour, if only for a few weeks, but cannot enjoy this experience because of the expense. There should be some way around this situation.

I haven't anything really concrete to offer, but a scheme might be evolved whereby a player who has been chosen for a specified number of M.C.C. tours should be entitled, as some small reward for his services to the game, to have his wife's return fare paid at least once. It would be up to the player to decide which tour.

Since the war I have spent six winters abroad. Len Hutton is the only other English cricketer who has done the same. So I think I can claim that he and I have done our fair share of travelling in the interests of English cricket. I also feel that it gives me the right to suggest that after a certain number of tours, a player should be offered the privilege of a free passage for his wife to join him—on the next tour. If he is not chosen for that tour, well, that's just too bad, but surely the prospect of a trip overseas for his wife will provide him with the incentive to earn a place in the team ?

I am not asking favours for myself or anyone else, but such an offer would do something to compensate the player for all the time he is away from home, for, believe me, the Test cricketer does spend a tremendous amount of time away from his home, his wife and children.

I am not complaining. I chose to be a County cricketer, but facts are facts, and they must be stated if we are to form a true picture of the situation.

I know that Len Hutton feels as I do on this point.
It is most unfair that a player with long Test service
should be prevented from having his wife with him for
a short time on one of his trips overseas just because he
cannot afford it. Mind you, I could not afford to have
Jean join me in the West Indies and Australia, but I made
sacrifices in my personal expenses, so that she could spend
a few weeks with me in both countries. I am not sorry I
did so. I only wish the wives of all players could enjoy
the same experience.

There is another point on the matter of incentive.
Several times during recent years we have had players
turning down the offer of a winter tour. This was the
case with some of the possible members of the recent trip
to India. Yet I am quite certain that if players with
five or six Test tours to their credit had known their wives
would be joining them later in the winter, this would have
been a decided incentive. A good thing for them—a
good thing for the M.C.C.—a good thing for India—
and a very good thing for cricket in general.

You may think that selection for an M.C.C. touring
side should be incentive enough, but there is not the same
fascination about a trip to one of the smaller Commonwealth countries that there is in, shall we say, a visit to
Australia. The thought of one's wife being given the opportunity of a winter holiday would make all the difference,
and players would be itching to go on the smaller tours.

I make no apologies for writing at such length about
the expenses side of this controversial subject, but I have
decided views and I feel it does one good to air one's personal opinions, providing, of course, that they are offered
in the right spirit. So please do not misunderstand me.
I am not making demands—I should be the last one to do
that. I am merely offering my own views and my suggestions, because I believe that this whole question of
wives on tour will have to be tackled sooner or later in the
right quarters.

I think the question is appreciated to a certain degree
by the M.C.C. Their attitude, however, is that if they

spend money on fares for players' wives, they will be depriving the Counties—particularly the rather poorer counties, who have been hard put to it during recent seasons to make ends meet—of part of the remuneration they might expect from profits made by the M.C.C. on tour. I can fully appreciate that point of view, but I still feel it is only part and not the whole answer. Perhaps it would be a good idea for the County secretaries to be given the opportunity to state their views on this subject. The matter does need the most careful thought, and every point of view must be explored.

Perhaps I should make myself clear on one point. It is this. I do not advocate that EVERY member of a side should take his wife on tour. Nor do I suggest for one moment that any player should be allowed to have his wife with him for the whole tour. That would be too big a responsibility for all concerned. Players are chosen to go on tour to play cricket, and to create friendships among the people of the country in which they are travelling and playing. But when a player had his wife with him he would naturally expect to give her a considerable amount of his leisure time, and that would not be right or fair to the rest of the party.

When players are together on tour, their associations off the field are reflected to some degree in their team spirit on the field, and this spirit might be spoiled if a number of wives were present throughout the whole tour.

As you know, those of us who have been fortunate enough to be joined by our wives did not have their company until nearly the end of the Test series, and that is a very different thing.

In any case, there is the wives' point of view. During a tour, players are expected to attend certain official functions, often for men only. On these occasions the wives would have to be left on their own, and if this happened too often, they might find the trip—if of too long duration—become irksome, and they, too, would soon begin to suffer home-sickness. That would do the players no good, either.

No, the answer is for wives to join their husbands towards the end of the tour, when the players themselves can begin to relax, or for a few weeks during the middle of the trip. That would be ideal for all concerned. At the moment, however, the wives of touring cricketers have little opportunity of spending even a few weeks with their husbands, mainly because of the expense involved in travelling to far-distant lands.

Should wives be allowed to join their cricketer husbands ? Should the authorities help to make it possible ? It is certainly a controversial subject. I have given you my frank views, and I leave them with you.

CHAPTER XVII

What of the Future?

THERE HAS BEEN A GREAT DEAL OF COMMENT DURING recent months concerning the future of County cricket in this country. In view of the struggle which many of the less-wealthy Counties are having each season to achieve financial stability, it is quite obvious that something will have to be done, and I should like to offer a few suggestions.

Let me say right away that I am convinced the game itself does not need altering in any way. Cricket is still the greatest of all games. No, it is the tempo of cricket that needs careful attention if the Counties are to attract the crowds back into their grounds.

How is this to be done? Well, I am quite certain that we play too much cricket in this country. At the same time, I do not advocate any curtailment of the number of fixtures in the County Championship programme. Then how can we reduce the amount of cricket played, you ask? By the playing of two 2-day matches each week— the first on Saturday and Sunday, the second on Wednesday and Thursday.

Does that sound revolutionary to you? Well, let me amplify my suggestion. First of all, the playing of 2-day matches will considerably speed up the tempo of the games. Points would be gained only for an outright win. There would be none whatever for a draw, not even for first innings points. This would mean that teams would have to go all out for victory in two days. Batsmen would be forced to attack to score runs as quickly as possible, and bowlers would not dare adopt negative tactics. Their business would be to get the other chaps out as quickly as they could, to give their own batsmen a chance to go for victory.

Saturday and Sunday would attract very good gates, I am certain of that, while the mid-week dates, one of which would be the early-closing day in that particular district, would also draw quite attractive crowds. In any case, there would be no wasted third days, which few people attend nowadays anyway.

The spare days in the week would not be wasted so far as the players are concerned. They would allow more time for travel, which at the moment is most inconvenient, and is often the cause of players being out of form, because they are tired out after all-night journeys. Then, surely, vacant days during the week could be used by players to engage in necessary practice in their own particular sphere.

What is even more important in these days, however, is that players would have time to carry on another job of some sort, or to attend to their private business commitments—very necessary owing to the high cost of living. It is surely obvious that if a player is engaged with his County for only two or perhaps three days a week, to allow for travelling, he could supplement his income and build up a career or business in readiness for the time when he would have to hang up his boots and gloves for the last time. This is something that must be faced, for few cricketers—even those in the top bracket—can afford to live only on their earnings from the game.

Two-day matches would also allow international players a certain amount of time at home with their families, which they do not get at the moment. This applies particularly to the young cricketer just setting up home. It has always seemed unfair to me that young married couples should be parted for such long periods as is the case when a young player reaches the top bracket of international cricket.

I repeat, that my suggestion for 2-day matches would not cause any reduction in the County programme. In fact, the fixture list could be extended to 32 matches, so that each County could play all the other Counties twice, which is not possible under the 3-day match policy. A

32-match programme would still allow players to obtain the rest they need from the present strain of constant cricket, with little respite.

In this connection I can state my own personal case. I am often criticised in Kent because people say I only pull out my best in Test cricket, but surely that is natural. I contend that no international player can be expected to keep up top form throughout a whole English season. I play to a plan, whether batting or keeping wicket. That plan sometimes breaks down—and not through any deliberate intent on my part. But although there are times when I fail with the bat, that does not mean that I am not trying.

I look at it this way. Is it better for me to strive for runs and neglect my wicket-keeping—or rather keep wicket indifferently, and perhaps lose my Test place? No! I feel I would sooner do my job well as a wicket-keeper for County and country than score 1,500 runs. There are plenty of players who can score 1,500 runs, but few who can keep wicket. But to do the *two* jobs equally well for six days a week, right through the season, Test matches as well, is, to my mind, impossible.

I am certain, however, that if we played only two 2-day matches each week, leaving spare time for other things, interest would be sharpened, and concentration strengthened. I know I am not alone in this contention, and such is my interest in cricket, the game I have made my profession, that I am anxious for something to be done about it. You see, I prefer to be master of one trade than Jack-of-all-trades. Cricket means too much to me for that.

I come now to another of my suggestions for creating new interest in the game. With spare days due to the playing of 2-day County games, it would be possible to organise a cricket cup. Again, 2-day matches, maybe on Monday and Tuesday, or Thursday and Friday. You may feel that this would kill my first plan, but actually it would do no such thing. After all, cup matches would not be played every week. Even if there was

one cup-tie sandwiched between two County games, this
would still leave a spare day in the week for other
purposes.

But I want to take it further than that. A cup competition, rather on the lines of the F.A. Cup, would give
chances to the Minor Counties, and even to the better-
class club sides. Why not ? Smaller clubs play in the
F.A. Cup, even if only in the earlier rounds, and these
matches create terrific local interest. They would do the
same to cricket.

Imagine the excitement and interest that would follow
the pairing of a club team against a County side, or even
a Minor Counties eleven. What a thrill it would be to
the players of the lesser-known side. Try to picture yourself as a young player perhaps batting against a Test star,
and doing well ; what encouragement it would give you to
achieve greater things. I am convinced that such matches
would lift the whole standard of cricket throughout the
country, and, incidentally, help the Counties in their
search for players.

I should like to see Scotland brought into this scheme,
too. The few players and clubs North of the Border are
more enthusiastic than anywhere else in Britain, but
because of a lack of competitive opportunity, the game
does not make the progress it should—and could. That
is one very good reason why Scotland would no doubt
welcome the institution of a cricket cup.

Another question often put to me concerns the importation of players from the Commonwealth. The form-
ation of the cup competition I have outlined might obviate
the necessity for Counties to seek players from beyond
their own borders, but at the moment, I cannot see any
alternative open to the smaller Counties but to recruit
players from other sources.

It is pleasing to know, however, that the M.C.C. have
done a very good job in this connection. The stronger
Counties usually have a surfeit of good players, and, in
consequence, there are always some who cannot hold
down a place in the County eleven. In many of these

cases recently, the M.C.C. have sanctioned special registrations, allowing home-bred players to change their Counties and to play for their new County without the usual qualification period.

Not so with players recruited from overseas. Here there is a three-years qualification rule. Not that I would stop good players coming into our game from the Commonwealth countries, but it is a good and wise policy to apply the registration rule, for this does give more opportunity to young players from this country. If the overseas importation was allowed to go straight into the team of his adopted County, chances for home lads would be even more limited than they are.

My next point may cause considerable controversy—it is that I would like to see all first-class cricketers classed as players, and not as amateurs or professionals, according to their status in the game. Each player would be paid a specified amount for each match, whether he wanted it or not. The man who wished to remain an " amateur " could always hand it to his pet charity.

Today there are a number of County appointments, such as assistant-secretary, which enable the holder of such an appointment to be classed as an amateur, when, really, he is just a player, even though he may be the captain of the side. Then again, some County clubs pay firms to employ a person so that he can continue to rank as an amateur. This is ridiculous—ludicrous, in fact. In such cases as this, I do honestly feel that the name " amateur " should be forgotten, because such a man is not an amateur as we know the term. To class all cricketers as players would obviate all the controversy that ensues on this question. If a man was capable of fulfilling another position with a County—secretary or assistant-secretary, for instance—then he would be paid accordingly, in addition to his playing fees. Surely that would be the fairest way.

Then again, in some sports the amateur is not allowed to give his name to advertisements, to write books, contribute newspaper columns and articles, or to coach for fees, but today there are amateurs in cricket doing just those things. Where's the sense of it ? Let's call us all players, and then we can do as we wish.

I am always hearing complaints from spectators that the Counties do not pay sufficient attention to the paying public. I am inclined to agree, and I feel that something must be done about this angle, too, if gates are to improve. Far be it from me to suggest that cricket should become a travelling circus, but I feel that there is a great need for some amenity or attraction to be provided to which spectators can turn for an hour or so as a break from the cricket, or when, as so often happens during most matches, the play becomes dull and uninteresting, or marred by rain. Why not make arrangements for two or three of the star players, who are not on the field—maybe because they have batted or are only the tail-enders—to go to a marquee erected to one side of the field, to give demonstrations to the youngsters.

You may say that this is a slur on the star, because he is not watching the game, or taking an interest in the play. But remember, I qualified my statement by saying " an uninteresting part of the game ". The marquee would be closely adjacent to the ring, and if the game should reach an interesting phase, it would be difficult to keep anyone inside the marquee—including the players. In any case, it is wrong to assume that players not batting sit and watch the game right through. They are human beings, after all. They read books (we get precious little spare time, you know !)—some play cards—there are letters to write—autograph books to be signed—while some of us like to spend these odd moments talking to friends and companions about matters entirely irrelevant to cricket.

So as it is a fact that players do not always sit watching the play in progress, why shouldn't some of them go to the marquee to show the younger generation how to develop their strokes, or their bowling—or even their fielding ? I am sure the players would not be averse to augmenting their income, especially if they knew they were interesting the youngsters. And not only the youngsters, either. What about the adults who never really have a chance to see at close-up, or talk to, the stars they so love ?

I am rather in favour of extending this business—and having a coco-nut shy. Don't let that shock you ! After all, there is nothing better to help a youngster to improve his fielding than throwing—and how much more keen he would be if there was a coco-nut to aim at. I said earlier that I do not wish to suggest that County cricket games be turned into circuses, and I repeat it, but if things were run on proper lines, with the cricket as the major attraction, understand, I feel that small sideshows that appertain to some phase of cricket, and to the increasing of interest in the game, would do good. They could do no less. For, let's face it, only the real enthusiast at a cricket match does not, at some time, lose interest in the play.

My marquee suggestion would also do something to avoid much of the tedious, irksome waiting about during showery weather, when the pitch assumes a very empty look. What happens now when rain stops play ? There is a frantic rush to the small tea tents, seldom big enough to shelter all those who try to crowd into them. Eventually, a large percentage of the paying spectators wend their way home, fed-up, and many of them do not patronise cricket again, maybe for a long time. Can you wonder at it ? But if there was another interest to hold them, would they not show their appreciation by their continued support ?

Although I stated in my opening sentences in this chapter that I found little wrong with the actual playing of cricket, perhaps I could make one suggestion, which, I am certain, would help to dispel some of the oft-voiced criticism of dull play. It concerns the later batsmen in the order.

I feel that when there is no occasion for Nos. 9, 10 and 11 to occupy the crease for long periods in an effort to stave off defeat or to " play for time ", when runs scored do not matter, then I suggest that captains should give orders that they are to get on with the game as quickly as possible. There is nothing more irritating than to see tail-enders, for no real reason at all, prodding about at the wicket, wasting time and scoring little. On the other hand, there is nothing more exhilarating than to see virtually a non-batter come to the wicket and start clouting the bowling all over the place.

If this happened more often we should see once again the recognised sloggers who were such colourful characters in cricket before the war—men like Alan Watt, of Kent ; in a much greater degree Arthur Wellard, of Somerset, and, of course, Jim Smith, of Middlesex. It is a fact that when " Big Jim " walked out to bat at Lord's, all the spectators in the refreshment rooms and bars immediately rushed back to watch the cricket. Crowds at Worcester, too, loved to see Reg Perks going out to bat, for they knew he would be out first ball or else slog a couple of glorious sixes—or even more !

Let's see this happen again. It could return, if only the County captains would show more enterprise in dictating the policy of the later batsmen. The crowds love action.

My last point—it concerns autograph hunting. I, like all other cricketers, would never deliberately disappoint any youngster who asks for an autograph, yet there are times when this gets a bit out of hand. I suggest, therefore, that this should be put on a proper and fair basis, and some system devised whereby everyone who genuinely wanted an autograph could get one.

I should like to see a scheme started whereby autograph hunters should be told to send their books to the County Secretary, together with a fee—no stated fee, just as much as can be afforded, even though it is only a penny or twopence. All moneys thus collected could be handed over to the Playing Fields Association. In this way not only would autographs be properly appreciated—I am afraid that many of the scraps of paper which we now sign are lost or thrown away—and the youngsters, by means of their small fee, would be helping to

provide themselves with fields to play in.   What is more,
I think you will agree, that something that has to be paid
for, even though it is only a matter of pence, is always
better prized and treasured.

Just a few suggestions, but I hope some of them will
find you in agreement.   I am all for improving our great
game, and will do anything I can to make this possible.

So here's to better cricket—and the more action the
better !

Index

221